LEGITIMATE DISTRUST

Book Two of *The Collapse of Trust* series

Why Conspiracy Theories Grow When Institutions Fail

Sebastian Saviano

STATERA PRESS

2026

Legitimate Distrust

Why Conspiracy Theories Grow When Institutions Fail

This is Book Two of The Collapse of Trust series.
(See full series listing on page v.)

Published by Statera Press
New York NY

ISBNs:
Hardcover: 979-8-9992336-6-0
Paperback: 979-8-9992336-5-3
e-Book: 979-8-9992336-4-6

Library of Congress Control Number **(LCCN):** 2026940038

For inquiries or permissions, visit:
www.SebastianSaviano.com

Printed in the United States of America and in select international locations.

This book is a work of historical research and informed analysis. While every effort has been made to ensure accuracy, the author and publisher assume no responsibility for errors, omissions, or any consequences arising from its use.

For those who kept asking questions
when easy answers were offered.

TABLE OF CONTENTS

Between doubt and belief, we still have to walk forward.

PREFACE

I did not set out to write a book about conspiracy theories.

I set out to understand a feeling I kept encountering—in public discourse, in private conversations, and, if I'm honest, in myself. A sense that something didn't quite add up. Not always in dramatic ways. Often in small ones: explanations that felt incomplete, institutions that couldn't quite account for themselves, moments where the official story wasn't obviously false, but didn't feel fully convincing either.

What struck me was how quickly that feeling was dismissed. The explanation was always the same: misinformation, polarization, irrationality. The problem, we were told, was that people had stopped thinking clearly.

That never seemed sufficient.

Over time, I became less interested in why people believe strange things, and more interested in why official explanations so often fail to satisfy. Because when they do, people don't stop trying to make sense of the world. They look elsewhere.

This book begins there.

It does not defend conspiratorial thinking, and it does not treat all skepticism as justified. Some beliefs are false, some harmful, some detached from reality. But dismissing all distrust as irrational misses something more important: the conditions under which distrust forms.

When institutions are opaque, inconsistent, or insulated from consequence, suspicion does not appear out of nowhere. It grows. Sometimes it remains grounded. Sometimes it drifts. Sometimes it hardens. But it rarely begins as pure delusion.

That realization changed the question for me.

The issue is not simply what people believe. It is whether the systems they are asked to trust can still explain themselves in ways that feel coherent and accountable.

This book is an attempt to think that through.

It also tries to hold a difficult line. On one side is dismissal—the view that distrust is a failure of citizens. On the other is surrender—the belief that all authority is corrupt and nothing can be trusted. Both, I think, are mistakes.

Distrust can be justified. It can also become corrosive.

We are not going back to a world of easy trust. Too much has changed. The more realistic question is what it means to live—and govern—when trust is partial, conditional, and often withheld.

That is the problem this book takes seriously.

It is written for readers who feel that tension: skeptical, but not cynical; critical, but not ready to abandon the possibility of shared reality. My aim is not to tell you what to believe, but to clarify what happens when trust breaks—and what it might take to make it possible again.

Sebastian Saviano

INTRODUCTION

Legitimate Distrust

Public discussions of conspiracy belief often begin from a diagnosis of irrationality. They focus on cognitive bias, misinformation, social media dynamics, or the psychological needs of believers. From this perspective, distrust appears as a defect—an error in reasoning to be corrected, managed, or contained. The underlying assumption is that institutions are broadly functional and that the primary problem lies with citizens who have lost the capacity to tell truth from falsehood.

This book begins from a different premise. It asks what conditions make distrust reasonable.

Across contemporary democracies, large numbers of people no longer accept official explanations at face value. They question institutional motives, doubt expertise, and interpret authority through suspicion rather than confidence. These reactions are often dismissed as dangerous, corrosive, or symptomatic of a "post-truth" age. Yet such labels do little to explain why mistrust has become so widespread, persistent, and resistant to correction.

The argument developed here is simple, but demanding: conspiracy belief is rarely the root problem. It is more often a secondary adaptation to environments in which authority no longer explains itself clearly, answers for its failures, or aligns power with accountability. When institutions become opaque, defensive, or insulated from consequence, distrust is not an anomaly. It is a rational response to exclusion from meaning-making.

This does not mean all suspicions are justified, nor that all alternative explanations are equal. It means that belief cannot be separated from the institutional conditions under which it forms. People are repeatedly asked to accept conclusions without access to reasoning, to defer to expertise without visibility into process, or to trust systems that do not acknowledge error. Under these pressures, skepticism becomes a form of self-protection rather than deviance.

The central claim of this book is therefore not that people have become incapable of trust, but that institutions have become less trustworthy in visible ways. Over time, small failures accumulate. Explanations grow thinner. Accountability becomes symbolic. Authority relies more on assertion than on visible justification. In such environments, belief migrates elsewhere—not necessarily because alternative narratives are more accurate, but because they feel more complete, coherent, and responsive to lived experience.

Understanding distrust in this way requires shifting attention away from individual psychology and toward institutional behavior. It requires examining how power is exercised, how decisions are communicated, and how responsibility is distributed when things go wrong. It also requires resisting the temptation to pathologize citizens for responding to conditions they did not create.

This book unfolds in three distinct movements.

The first section is diagnostic. It examines how distrust forms under contemporary institutional conditions and how it evolves from episodic skepticism into durable belief. These chapters do not treat conspiracy thinking as a psychological anomaly, but as a patterned response to repeated experiences of opacity, inconsistency, and consequence without accountability. The goal is to show how mistrust becomes rationalized—not because every suspicion is correct, but because explanatory authority weakens over time.

Midway through this diagnostic arc, Chapter 6, *Shadows That Stay*, isolates a recurring intuition: the perception that power persists beyond electoral turnover and operates without meaningful consent. Often described colloquially as the "deep state," this perception is frequently dismissed in its most elaborate forms. This chapter neither endorses nor debunks such claims. Instead, it examines why the sense of enduring, self-protective authority remains compelling across ideological lines, separating structural continuity from speculative narrative.

An interlude titled *Moral Grammars and the Preconditions of Trust* follows. This is not a transition to reform but a conceptual excavation. It asks what implicit moral expectations govern the relationship between authority and citizen in the first place. Trust does not rest only on performance; it depends on shared assumptions about fairness, reciprocity, visibility, and restraint. When these underlying moral grammars fracture, institutional failure is experienced not as error but as betrayal. Naming these preconditions prepares the analysis to move from diagnosis to structural comparison.

The second movement of the book is comparative and structural. It examines how mistrust manifests across different institutional designs and political arrangements. Rather than treating conspiracism as uniquely American or technologically driven, these chapters show how similar structural pressures—continuity of power, administrative insulation, informational asymmetry— produce distinct patterns of suspicion depending on how authority is organized and justified. This comparative lens clarifies what is systemic rather than cultural.

The final movement turns toward reconstruction. It asks not how to persuade citizens to trust again, but what institutional practices could render authority worthy of conditional belief. These chapters reject nostalgia for pre-digital legitimacy and instead confront a harder reality: generalized civic trust may not return. The question is therefore how institutions can operate credibly under conditions of persistent skepticism. Transparency, contestability, visible restraint, and accountable continuity emerge not as rhetorical commitments but as structural requirements.

At the same time, this book rejects the fantasy of full restoration. Trust, as a generalized civic posture, is unlikely to return in the form many institutions still expect. Legitimacy must function without confidence. Authority must operate even when it is doubted. The task is not to eliminate skepticism, but to prevent it from becoming corrosive enough to collapse shared reality altogether.

This reframing carries implications for both institutions and citizens. Institutions are not entitled to belief, but they remain obligated to explain themselves, admit uncertainty, accept consequence, and remain contestable. Citizens are not required to trust, but they are not released from responsibility. Skepticism can be justified without becoming absolute. Doubt can be principled without becoming nihilistic.

Throughout, the book insists on a careful distinction: distrust is not the same as disengagement, and suspicion is not the same as negation. When grounded and disciplined, mistrust can function as a civic signal—a demand for better systems rather than the rejection of systems altogether. When ignored, dismissed, or exploited, it becomes a resource for manipulation.

This book is not a defense of conspiracy belief, nor an indictment of democratic governance. It is an attempt to take mistrust seriously without surrendering to it. The chapters that follow trace how distrust is produced, how it spreads, and how it hardens. They aim to clarify what has broken between citizens and authority, and what must change if shared reality is to remain possible.

The argument does not promise resolution. It offers clarity. And it begins from the conviction that trust is not what institutions ask for, but what they build—through conduct, under scrutiny, and in plain sight.

A Note on Terms

This book uses several recurring concepts to describe the relationship between institutions and citizens. These terms are not meant to be technical or exclusive. They are offered as tools for clarity. The definitions below are working descriptions used consistently throughout the chapters that follow.

Accountability. Accountability means that authority faces meaningful consequence when it fails. Symbolic acknowledgment without structural correction does not restore credibility.

Continuity of Power. Continuity of power refers to the persistence of institutional actors, practices, or agendas across changes in leadership. Continuity can provide stability. It can also generate suspicion when citizens perceive that electoral turnover does not meaningfully affect decision-making.

Distrust. Distrust is not the absence of trust, but a shift in posture. It reflects heightened vigilance toward authority, often grounded in repeated experiences of opacity, inconsistency, or unacknowledged error. Distrust becomes corrosive only when it hardens into total negation.

Explanatory Authority. Explanatory authority refers to the ability of institutions to provide accounts of decisions and outcomes that are intelligible, credible, and open to scrutiny. It is not merely the power to assert conclusions, but the capacity to make those conclusions understandable and contestable.

Legitimacy. Legitimacy is the shared belief that an institution has the right to exercise power. It depends not only on legal authorization but on visible justification, restraint, and accountability.

Opacity. Opacity refers to decision-making processes that are difficult for outsiders to see, evaluate, understand, or contest. Some opacity is inevitable in complex systems. Persistent opacity, however, weakens confidence and invites suspicion.

Reciprocity. Reciprocity describes the expectation that institutions recognize citizens not merely as subjects of policy but as participants in shared governance. When reciprocity weakens, institutional failure is often experienced as betrayal rather than error.

Structural Pressures. Throughout the book, "structural" refers to patterns embedded in institutional design rather than the motives of individual actors. Structural pressures shape behavior even when intentions differ.

Trust. Trust refers to the willingness to rely on authority without constant verification. It does not require agreement with every decision. It requires a baseline belief that institutions act within recognizable limits and remain responsive to consequence.

These definitions are not offered to settle debate, but to clarify how the terms function within this argument. The goal of this book is not to redefine trust or mistrust in abstract terms, but to examine how institutional conduct shapes whether either posture becomes reasonable.

On Epistemology and "the Epistemic"

Throughout this book, the terms *epistemology* and *epistemic* are used to describe how knowledge is formed, justified, and recognized as credible.

Epistemology, in its simplest sense, asks: *How do we know what we claim to know?* It concerns the processes by which claims are evaluated, evidence is weighed, and authority is granted or withheld.

When this book refers to *epistemic conditions* or *epistemic environments*, it is describing the structures through which knowledge becomes visible or obscured—how decisions are explained, how evidence is presented, and how institutions make their reasoning accessible or inaccessible to the public.

Distrust, in this framework, is not only a political or psychological response. It is an epistemic one. It reflects a breakdown in the conditions under which knowledge can be evaluated, shared, and trusted.

Understanding mistrust therefore requires attention not only to what people believe, but to how systems make belief possible—or impossible— in the first place.

CHAPTER 1

Through the Lens of Others

Understanding the Conspiracy Debate

This chapter begins by situating *Legitimate Distrust* within the existing scholarly and public conversations about conspiracy theories. Before turning to institutional behavior, historical betrayal, or questions of repair, it is necessary to understand how conspiracy belief has most commonly been interpreted, studied, and evaluated—and what assumptions quietly structure those interpretations.

Across psychology, sociology, political science, and media studies, conspiracy theories are typically approached as problems of belief. The central question is not what such narratives reveal about the systems they contest, but why certain individuals or groups come to accept explanations that diverge from official or expert accounts. Researchers have emphasized cognitive bias, emotional reasoning, social alienation, political polarization, and information disorder as primary drivers of conspiratorial thinking. While these approaches differ in method and emphasis, they share a common analytic orientation: belief itself is treated as the primary site of dysfunction.

This focus has produced valuable insights. It has clarified how uncertainty amplifies pattern-seeking, how identity and belonging shape credibility judgments, and how contemporary media environments intensify suspicion. Yet this body of work also establishes the boundaries of its own inquiry. By centering belief as the object to be explained, it often leaves less examined the broader conditions under which distrust becomes plausible, persistent, or widely shared—particularly in contexts marked by institutional opacity, historical deception, or repeated failures of accountability.

The purpose of this chapter is not to dismiss existing research, nor to suggest that all forms of suspicion are justified. Rather, it is to map the dominant frames through which conspiracy belief has been understood and to identify the questions those frames tend to sidestep. Doing so prepares the ground for a shift in emphasis that unfolds over the chapters that follow—one that gradually moves from the psychology of belief toward the structures, practices, and moral expectations that shape public trust.

This chapter, then, functions as orientation rather than argument. It outlines how the conspiracy debate has been framed, where those frames have proven most useful, and where they appear insufficient for understanding the durability of contemporary mistrust. The analytic turn this book proposes is introduced here only in outline. Its implications—and its limits— are developed later, as the focus shifts from belief as an object of explanation to institutions as agents of interpretation.

I. How Conspiracy Belief Is Commonly Studied

Scholars across psychology, sociology, political science, and media studies have approached conspiracy belief from different angles, but they tend to begin in the same place: by asking why people accept explanations that diverge from official or expert accounts. The central concern is belief—how it forms and persists.[1]

Psychological research has been especially influential in shaping this view. Within that literature, conspiracy belief is often linked to cognitive tendencies that become more pronounced under conditions of uncertainty or threat. Studies suggest that when individuals experience a loss of control, they are more likely to perceive patterns in random or ambiguous events.[2] These mechanisms are ordinarily adaptive for navigating risk. But when events feel chaotic or poorly explained, they can produce narratives that impose order where clarity is lacking. From this perspective, conspiracy theories offer explanatory closure and a sense of control in environments perceived as unstable.[3]

Sociological approaches emphasize a different, though complementary, set of dynamics. Rather than focusing on individual cognition, these accounts situate conspiracy belief within broader experiences of alienation, marginalization, and social dislocation. Here, conspiratorial narratives are interpreted as expressions of estrangement from political, economic, or cultural institutions that no longer appear responsive or representative. Belief is shaped not only by how people think, but by where they are positioned within social hierarchies and networks of power.[4]

A third major strand of research emerges from political science and media studies, where conspiracy theories are analyzed in relation to populism, polarization, and information disorder. Scholars working in this tradition examine how conspiratorial narratives are mobilized by political actors, amplified by fragmented media ecosystems, and sustained through algorithmic incentives that reward outrage and certainty over complexity. In these accounts, conspiracy belief is less a private psychological response than a public political phenomenon—one that can be strategically cultivated and weaponized.[5]

Cultural critics such as Charles P. Pierce have framed conspiracy thinking less as a cognitive puzzle than as a civic failure—an outcome of degraded media ecosystems, political opportunism, and the monetization of irresponsibility, in which skepticism becomes detached from shared standards of truth and accountability.[6] This critique usefully documents the conditions under which conspiratorial narratives flourish, but it tends to treat distrust itself as a defect to be corrected, rather than as a response requiring institutional explanation.

Related work in media and cultural studies examines conspiracy narratives as cultural forms shaped by secrecy, power, and epistemic instability.[7]

These frameworks differ in their explanatory focus, but they share several underlying assumptions. Most treat conspiracy belief as a departure from epistemic norms—something that arises when reasoning fails, information breaks down, or social trust erodes beyond a tolerable threshold. Suspicion, in this view, is not inherently illegitimate, but it is something to be managed, corrected, or redirected back toward institutional authority. The analytic task is to identify the sources of distortion and reduce their influence.

It is important to note that this orientation is neither monolithic nor uniformly dismissive. Many scholars acknowledge that real conspiracies have occurred, that institutional deception has a documented history, and that distrust can emerge from lived experience rather than mere fantasy. Some explicitly caution against pathologizing all forms of skepticism. Nevertheless, the dominant emphasis remains on belief as the primary object of concern, with comparatively less attention paid to the conditions that render official explanations fragile or unconvincing.

This chapter proceeds from the recognition that this literature has described important features of conspiratorial belief while leaving certain structural questions underdeveloped. Understanding how conspiracy theories are commonly studied is a necessary first step—not because these accounts are wrong, but because their shared assumptions shape the limits of what they can explain.

II. Where These Approaches Reach Their Limits

The frameworks outlined above have substantially advanced our understanding of conspiracy belief, yet their explanatory power is not without limits. These limits do not stem from carelessness or oversight. They follow from the starting assumptions that shape which questions are asked first—and which are left for later.

One such blind spot concerns the role of historical experience. While many accounts acknowledge that real conspiracies and institutional deceptions have occurred—from Watergate to the Tuskegee syphilis study[8]—they rarely examine how verified episodes of deception shape the epistemic environment in which later claims are evaluated.[9] The legacy of past wrongdoing is often treated as background context rather than as an active force shaping how people judge credibility and authority today. As a result, the cumulative effects of deception across time—particularly within communities that have repeatedly experienced institutional harm—remain underexplored.

A second limitation involves institutional behavior itself. Much of the literature takes institutions as relatively stable reference points against which belief is measured: they may be imperfect, but they are presumed to function as default arbiters of legitimacy and truth. Less attention is paid to how institutional practices—such as secrecy, contradiction, delay, or strategic communication—shape the conditions under which knowledge is produced and evaluated. When institutions alter their narratives, withhold information, or speak in ways that appear inconsistent with lived experience, the epistemic consequences of those actions are seldom treated as objects of sustained analysis.

A further constraint appears in the treatment of tone and response. Dismissal, ridicule, and pathologizing language are often analyzed for their effects on belief persistence at the individual level, but less often for their broader political or social consequences. How authority responds to doubt—whether with engagement, correction, or contempt—may influence not only what people believe, but how they understand their relationship to power, expertise, and public discourse.

Taken together, these gaps point to a central tension within existing research. Frameworks focused primarily on cognition and misinformation can explain why individuals adopt certain beliefs in specific contexts, yet they struggle to account for patterns of mistrust that recur across time, class, and geography. When similar forms of skepticism emerge in markedly different cultural and political environments, purely psychological or informational models struggle to explain that pattern.

This observation does not suggest that conspiracy belief should be normalized or excused. Rather, it raises the possibility that belief itself may be less anomalous than commonly assumed. If so, the anomaly may lie not solely in how people think, but in the conditions under which they are asked to trust—conditions that remain insufficiently examined within prevailing approaches.

III. A Shift in Emphasis, Not a Rejection

The limits identified in the preceding discussion do not require abandoning existing research on conspiracy belief. Cognitive bias, emotional reasoning, and identity-driven interpretation remain essential components of how individuals make sense of complex and uncertain worlds.

This book builds on those insights, but begins from a different starting point. Rather than asking what may be wrong in how people think, it asks what may be changing in how institutions behave—and how those changes reshape the conditions under which belief and disbelief take hold.

This shift reorients the analysis toward distrust itself—not simply as an error to be corrected, but as a phenomenon to be examined.

Throughout this book, "epistemic" refers to the conditions that shape how people come to know what is true, whom they trust as credible, and why certain explanations feel convincing.

To adopt this posture is not to endorse every belief it produces, but to understand the conditions under which distrust becomes persuasive. At the center of this approach is a working hypothesis: some forms of mistrust arise from conditions that make skepticism reasonable, even when the conclusions people draw from that skepticism are not. In other words, when institutions have a history of opacity, inconsistency, or unacknowledged error, it can be reasonable for individuals to question official explanations. That skepticism, however, can extend beyond what the evidence supports. The resulting conclusions are often more certain or expansive than the available information justifies.

The aim here is diagnostic: to examine how institutional conduct, historical experience, and informational environments shape what feels credible before judging which conclusions are warranted.

This approach privileges curiosity over condemnation. It proceeds from the assumption that dismissing distrust as mere irrationality risks obscuring the forces that sustain it, while uncritical validation risks reinforcing its most destructive forms. Between these poles lies an analytic task that this book takes up.

IV. From Reframing to Structure

The chapters that follow take up this shift in emphasis, examining how the conditions under which belief forms have changed—and how those changes shape patterns of trust and distrust. They build incrementally, tracing how suspicion forms and becomes embedded in public life.

The analysis begins by examining how suspicion forms and spreads. It traces how individuals respond to uncertainty, contradiction, and perceived exclusion, and how these responses are reinforced through social and informational environments. From there, the focus widens to moments in which distrust was not merely imagined but earned. These episodes continue to influence expectations of authority long after their immediate causes have faded.

Subsequent chapters explore how secrecy, opacity, and institutional inconsistency alter the moral expectations placed on those who govern and inform. As these conditions persist, distinctions between reasonable skepticism and destructive paranoia become harder to maintain, and beliefs that once appeared marginal can take on broader appeal.

It then turns to the consequences of this progression. When distrust becomes systemic rather than episodic, it reshapes civic relationships, political behavior, and the shared foundations of public knowledge. The later chapters consider what it would mean to address these conditions—not by prescribing belief, but by examining the environments in which trust and distrust are produced.

The progression is deliberate. What begins as individual suspicion expands into institutional patterns and, ultimately, civic consequences. The aim is not to rush toward resolution, but to follow this escalation carefully, allowing each stage to illuminate the next.

Conclusion

This chapter has clarified how conspiracy belief has been framed, studied, and evaluated, while identifying the limits of those frameworks without dismissing their contributions.

The chapters that follow proceed from a simple assumption: neither ridicule nor romanticization offers much insight. Suspicion can distort reality, but it does not arise from nothing. Treating conspiracy belief solely as a cognitive error risks overlooking the environments in which doubt becomes persistent and difficult to dislodge.

Beginning in the next chapter, this book examines those environments. It does not begin with conclusions about who is right or wrong, but with questions about how trust is produced, strained, and withdrawn. The inquiry that follows is not an appeal for belief, but an effort to understand what belief now requires.

REFERENCES

1 Rob Brotherton, *Suspicious Minds: Why We Believe Conspiracy Theories* (Bloomsbury, 2015).

2 Jennifer A. Whitson and Adam D. Galinsky, "Lacking Control Increases Illusory Pattern Perception," *Science* 322, no. 5898 (October 3, 2008), https://doi.org/10.1126/science.1159845

3 Jan-Willem van Prooijen, *The Psychology of Conspiracy Theories* (Routledge, 2018).

4 Jaron Harambam, *Contemporary Conspiracy Culture: Truth and Knowledge in an Era of Epistemic Instability* (Routledge, 2020).

5 Nancy L. Rosenblum and Russell Muirhead, *A Lot of People Are Saying: The New Conspiracism and the Assault on Democracy* (Princeton University Press, 2019); Yochai Benkler, Robert Faris, and Hal Roberts, *Network Propaganda: Manipulation, Disinformation, and Radicalization in American Politics* (Oxford University Press, 2018).

6 Charles P. Pierce, *Idiot America: How Stupidity Became a Virtue in the Land of the Free* (Doubleday, 2009).

7 Mark Fenster, *Conspiracy Theories: Secrecy and Power in American Culture* (University of Minnesota Press, 2008).

8 Kathryn S. Olmsted, *Real Enemies: Conspiracy Theories and American Democracy, World War I to 9/11* (Oxford University Press, 2009).

Suspicion rarely begins as ideology.
More often, it begins as discomfort.

CHAPTER 2

From Suspicion to System

The Psychology of Mistrust and the Sociology of Belief

Suspicion rarely begins as ideology. More often, it begins as discomfort—an unresolved tension between what one is told and what one observes, remembers, or feels to be true. An explanation is offered, but it does not settle the unease. Reassurance is given, but it feels incomplete. Over time, the gap between official narrative and personal perception does not close; it widens.

In its earliest form, suspicion is not a claim about hidden enemies or coordinated plots. It is a question: *Why doesn't this make sense?* That question is not inherently irrational. It reflects a basic human impulse to seek coherence in moments of uncertainty, contradiction, or threat. When events appear chaotic or explanations feel misaligned with lived experience, the mind searches for patterns, causes, and agency. Suspicion, at this stage, functions less as belief than as vigilance.

Psychological research has long recognized this impulse. Humans are pattern-seeking creatures, attuned to signs of danger and motivated to explain disruptions in their environment. In situations marked by ambiguity or loss of control, heightened attention to hidden causes can serve a protective function. Suspicion alerts us to the possibility that appearances are misleading and that important information may be missing. Far from being an immediate pathology, it is often an adaptive response to instability.

Yet suspicion does not remain purely individual for long. Questions circulate. Doubts are shared. Interpretations are compared. What begins as a private sense that "something doesn't add up" can become a shared orientation toward the world. As suspicion moves from the mind into social space, it acquires narrative structure, emotional reinforcement, and moral meaning. It becomes not just a response to uncertainty, but a way of interpreting it.

This chapter examines that progression. It traces how suspicion forms, how it is sustained through social interaction, and how it can harden into a durable worldview when reinforced by institutional behavior and collective experience. The aim is not to validate every belief that emerges from distrust, but to understand how mistrust takes shape under conditions that make it feel reasonable, coherent, and resistant to correction.

By grounding conspiracy belief in the emotional and social logic of suspicion, this chapter lays the foundation for a broader argument. Modern conspiracism is not reducible to individual irrationality. It emerges from the interaction between human psychology and the institutional conditions within which credibility is granted, withheld, or withdrawn. To understand how mistrust becomes systemic, one must first understand how it begins.

I. Suspicion as Reflex and Response

Psychological research helps clarify why suspicion emerges so readily under conditions of uncertainty or threat. Experimental studies suggest that when individuals experience a loss of control, they are more likely to perceive patterns in random or ambiguous events.[1] Humans look for agency behind events. We prefer explanations that match the scale of what has happened.[2] These instincts are usually adaptive. But when events feel chaotic, disempowering, or poorly explained, they can produce narratives that impose order where clarity is lacking. From this perspective, conspiracy theories offer closure and a sense of control in environments that feel unstable.[3]

Suspicion also develops within social position. Experiences of alienation, marginalization, or exclusion from political and economic power shape how individuals interpret authority.[4] Conspiratorial narratives can express estrangement from institutions that no longer appear responsive or representative. Belief reflects not only reasoning styles but lived relationships to authority.

Suspicion is further shaped by contemporary information systems. Political actors can mobilize conspiratorial rhetoric strategically, while fragmented media environments reward certainty, outrage, and simplified narratives.[5] In such contexts, conspiracy belief becomes not only a psychological response but a political instrument.

Taken together, these insights illuminate why suspicion arises and why it can persist. Yet when treated primarily as deviations in reasoning or trust, they risk overlooking how recurring institutional patterns shape the conditions under which suspicion appears reasonable. The question is not only why individuals believe, but why distrust finds such durable footing.

This body of work is neither simplistic nor uniformly dismissive. Many scholars acknowledge that real conspiracies have occurred and that institutions have deceived the public. Even so, the dominant focus remains on belief itself, with less sustained attention to the conditions that make official explanations appear fragile or unconvincing.

These accounts are not wrong. They clarify how conspiracy belief operates. But the questions they ask at the outset shape what they are able to see—and what they leave in the background.

II. The Social Life of Belief

Suspicion does not remain a private cognitive posture for long. Once articulated—shared with a friend, posted online, or exchanged within a community—it begins to take on social form. Doubts circulate, interpretations are compared, and isolated questions acquire collective meaning. What was once an individual sense that something "doesn't add up" becomes part of a shared way of seeing.

Beliefs formed under these conditions are sustained not only by evidence or argument, but by social reinforcement. Communities of interpretation provide validation, language, and emotional support. Within these spaces, skepticism is no longer experienced as alienation; it becomes belonging. The act of doubting together transforms uncertainty into solidarity, and suspicion into identity.

Narrative plays a central role in this process. Conspiratorial explanations offer coherence where events feel fragmented or contradictory. They connect disparate experiences into a single story with clear causal lines, restoring a sense of order in environments perceived as chaotic. In doing so, they often supply what official accounts lack: an explanation that feels complete, morally legible, and responsive to lived experience.

These narratives also tend to simplify moral complexity. By dividing the world into victims and perpetrators, insiders and outsiders, conspiracy frameworks provide clarity about who is to blame and where loyalty should lie. This moral structure can be emotionally satisfying, particularly in contexts where responsibility appears diffuse or unacknowledged. Ambiguity is replaced by conviction; confusion by certainty.

The social life of belief is further shaped by contemporary communication environments. Digital platforms allow suspicion to spread rapidly, connect across geographic distance, and persist through repetition. Reinforcement is not merely interpersonal but algorithmic, as emotionally charged interpretations receive greater visibility and circulation. Over time, exposure to similar narratives strengthens confidence, even in the absence of new information.

As suspicion becomes embedded within social relationships and shared narratives, it grows more resilient. Challenges from outside the community are more easily dismissed, not because they lack merit, but because they come from sources already deemed untrustworthy. At this stage, belief is no longer just a response to uncertainty; it is a social orientation that structures how information is received, evaluated, and remembered.

Understanding this social dimension is essential. Without it, conspiracy belief appears as an individual failure of reasoning. With it, belief can be seen as a collective process—one that satisfies emotional, moral, and relational needs that extend well beyond the content of any single claim.

III. Mistrust as Systemic, Not Merely Psychological

When suspicion persists, it rarely does so in isolation. Repeated encounters with contradiction, deflection, or denial begin to accumulate, altering how institutions themselves are perceived. What starts as a question about a single explanation can become a broader doubt about the system that produced it. The logic is not complex: if authority misled once, or appeared evasive when clarity was expected, why assume transparency the next time?

This shift marks an important transition. Suspicion is no longer directed at a discrete claim or event; it becomes generalized. Individuals move from asking *"Is this explanation incomplete?"* to wondering *"Is the system itself trustworthy?"* In this way, mistrust expands from a momentary reaction into a durable orientation toward power, expertise, and official knowledge.

Institutional behavior plays a critical role in this transformation. What matters in this process is not the severity of any single failure, but their accumulation. Mistrust rarely emerges from one contradiction alone. It is learned gradually, as institutions revise accounts without transparency, delay disclosure without explanation, or deflect responsibility across layers of authority. Over time, these patterns teach observers what to expect—not truth or falsehood in any given case, but evasiveness as a norm.

Once that expectation takes hold, credibility erodes preemptively, before any new claim is evaluated on its merits.

When accountability is absent, narratives change without acknowledgment, or responsibility is diffused across agencies and actors, uncertainty hardens into doubt. Explanations that might once have been accepted are reinterpreted through a lens of skepticism, not because alternative accounts have been proven, but because the system no longer appears answerable to those it governs.

Mistrust deepens further when institutional narratives conflict with lived experience. Discrepancies between public messaging and observable outcomes create a sense that reality is being managed rather than explained. This pattern appears across health, finance, security, and governance. When people feel that what they are told systematically fails to account for what they see or endure, suspicion becomes less about imagination and more about inference.

At this stage, mistrust begins to exhibit systemic qualities. It is shared, reinforced, and transmitted across social networks. It no longer requires a triggering event to be sustained; it becomes self-reinforcing. New information is filtered through existing doubt, and institutional reassurances are interpreted as further evidence of concealment or bad faith.

Understanding mistrust as systemic does not require assuming that institutions are uniformly deceptive or malicious. It requires recognizing that legitimacy depends not only on formal authority, but on consistent patterns of explanation, accountability, and responsiveness. When those patterns break down, mistrust is no longer an individual pathology. It is a rational response to perceived structural failure.

IV. When Suspicion Becomes a Belief System

Suspicion becomes a belief system when it no longer functions as a provisional stance toward uncertainty, but as a stable framework for interpreting reality. At this stage, doubt is no longer episodic or event-specific; it is generalized and anticipatory. New information is not evaluated on its own terms, but filtered through a settled expectation of deception.

One marker of this transition is the way institutional denial is received. When mistrust has become entrenched, official rebuttals do not resolve uncertainty; they intensify it. Statements intended to reassure are interpreted as evidence of concealment, and corrections are read as strategic reversals rather than good-faith clarification. The logic is internally consistent: if institutions are presumed deceptive, then denial itself confirms the suspicion it seeks to dispel.

As this logic stabilizes, individuals begin to detach from mainstream sources of authority and expertise. This is not experienced as withdrawal, but as emancipation. Believers come to see themselves as epistemically independent—no longer reliant on institutions they regard as compromised. Alternative sources of information gain credibility not because they meet conventional standards of verification, but because they are perceived as unaligned with dominant power structures.

Trust, under these conditions, becomes highly selective. It is extended horizontally rather than vertically—toward fellow skeptics, alternative media figures, or decentralized networks of interpretation. Agreement reinforces credibility, and shared doubt substitutes for institutional validation. What matters is not whether a claim is true in an absolute sense, but whether it fits within the existing interpretive framework.

At this point, conspiracy belief ceases to function as a collection of discrete claims and becomes a structural logic. The world is understood through inversion: if official accounts are presumed false, then their opposite feels closer to the truth. This does not require coordination or evidence of deception in every case. It requires only a consistent expectation that power conceals its true intentions.

Once suspicion hardens in this way, it becomes resistant to correction. Counterevidence is absorbed, reframed, or dismissed. This is not because believers are incapable of reasoning, but because the reasoning process itself is now governed by a different set of epistemic assumptions. Belief persists not through ignorance, but through coherence. The system holds because it explains why nothing else can be trusted.

Understanding this transformation is critical. It shows how suspicion, initially adaptive and responsive, can evolve into a self-sustaining worldview—one that is internally rational even as it becomes increasingly detached from shared standards of knowledge. The question that follows is not why such belief systems are difficult to dismantle, but what conditions allow them to form in the first place.

V. Psychological Theories: Useful, But Not Enough

Psychological research has offered some of the most influential explanations for conspiracy belief, and its contributions should not be minimized. Scholars have identified cognitive tendencies that help explain why conspiratorial narratives appeal during periods of uncertainty or threat. Among the most frequently discussed are proportionality bias—the intuition that significant events must have equally significant causes—and the desire to restore a sense of control when circumstances feel unstable.[6]

When outcomes appear too consequential to be accidental, explanations involving deliberate coordination can feel more satisfying than those invoking complexity or chance. Similarly, when individuals feel excluded from decision-making processes, conspiratorial narratives can provide a compensatory sense of agency.

Another line of research points to the discomfort created by ambiguity and incomplete information. Conspiracy theories reduce that discomfort by offering internally coherent stories that close explanatory gaps.[7] These accounts are empirically grounded and descriptively useful. They help explain why conspiratorial beliefs intensify during crises and why they recur across populations. Yet on their own, they frame belief primarily as a function of cognitive bias or emotional vulnerability. What they rarely address is why uncertainty, loss of control, or epistemic anxiety has become so widespread in the first place.

Without examining the environments that generate these conditions, psychological explanations remain incomplete.

VI. The Turn Toward Structural Suspicion

When the conditions that produce suspicion are widely shared, mistrust takes on a structural character. When large numbers of people encounter recurring contradictions, exclusions, or failures of explanation, doubt takes on a sociological character. It becomes less about individual disposition and more about patterned experience.

One driver of this shift is control over information. When the production or release of knowledge appears tightly managed, trust depends not only on accuracy but on perceived openness. Even correct information can fail to persuade if the process behind it feels opaque.

Another driver is the gap between institutional rhetoric and lived experience. When organizations speak in the language of transparency and responsibility but outcomes feel misaligned with those promises, credibility erodes. Repeated discrepancies between words and experience teach observers what to expect—not necessarily deception in every case, but defensiveness as a norm.

Communication style matters as well. Technical reassurance may be formally correct yet experientially disconnected. When explanations do not seem to recognize disruption, loss, or uncertainty as people encounter them, skepticism grows—not because expertise is rejected, but because it feels distant.

These dynamics help explain why similar forms of suspicion emerge across distinct domains. Whether the issue is public health, financial systems, or environmental policy, mistrust tends to grow where explanations appear insufficiently responsive to lived uncertainty.

The significance of this shift is not that institutions are always deceptive. It is that legitimacy is increasingly evaluated through experience rather than authority.[8] When systems repeatedly fail to account for what people see or endure, suspicion becomes a rational social posture.

VII. Key Takeaway

Suspicion becomes a system when systems are no longer believable. What begins as a cognitive response to uncertainty can harden into a durable worldview when reinforced by social validation and institutional failure. At that point, mistrust is no longer episodic or reactive; it is structured. It shapes how information is filtered, which sources are granted credibility, and which explanations are dismissed in advance. Belief persists not because individuals abandon reason, but because reason is reorganized around the expectation that authority conceals more than it reveals.

Under these conditions, conspiratorial thinking is best understood not as an anomaly of irrational minds, but as a predictable response to environments in which accountability is inconsistent, communication is opaque, and lived experience diverges from official narrative. Suspicion escalates not because critical thinking disappears, but because its foundations become unstable.

The implication is not that all mistrust is justified, nor that every alternative explanation deserves equal weight. It is that belief systems rooted in suspicion draw their strength from structural conditions that cannot be addressed by correction alone. When distrust becomes systemic, it reflects a breakdown in legitimacy rather than a failure of cognition.

This chapter has traced how that breakdown takes shape—moving from individual reflex, to social reinforcement, to structural orientation.

Conclusion

The chapters that follow move backward in time to examine how those conditions emerged. Before distrust became systemic, it was often earned. Understanding that history is essential—not to vindicate suspicion, but to clarify how credibility is lost, why it is difficult to restore, and what trust now demands in an environment shaped by its repeated erosion.

REFERENCES

1 Jennifer A. Whitson and Adam D. Galinsky, "Lacking Control Increases Illusory Pattern Perception," *Science* 322, no. 5898 (October 3, 2008), https://doi.org/10.1126/science.1159845.

2 Jan-Willem van Prooijen, *The Psychology of Conspiracy Theories* (Routledge, 2018).

3 Rob Brotherton, *Suspicious Minds: Why We Believe Conspiracy Theories* (Bloomsbury, 2015).

4 Jaron Harambam, *Contemporary Conspiracy Culture: Truth and Knowledge in an Era of Epistemic Instability* (Routledge, 2020).

5 Nancy L. Rosenblum and Russell Muirhead, *A Lot of People Are Saying: The New Conspiracism and the Assault on Democracy* (Princeton University Press, 2019); Yochai Benkler, Robert Faris, and Hal Roberts, *Network Propaganda: Manipulation, Disinformation, and Radicalization in American Politics* (Oxford University Press, 2018).

6 van Prooijen, *The Psychology of Conspiracy Theories*; Brotherton, *Suspicious Minds*.

7 Quassim Cassam, *Conspiracy Theories* (Polity Press, 2019).

8 Pierre Rosanvallon, *Counter-Democracy: Politics in an Age of Distrust* (Cambridge University Press, 2008).

CHAPTER 3

Historical Betrayals

Conspiracies That Were Proven True

The term *conspiracy theory* is often used as a diagnostic label—an indicator of cognitive failure, emotional instability, or susceptibility to misinformation. Yet this usage collapses an important distinction: between speculative belief and documented coordination. Not all conspiracies are theories. Some are historical facts that were once dismissed precisely because they challenged institutional credibility.

In these cases, the problem was not excessive suspicion, but premature trust.

Before declassification, whistleblowers, investigative journalism, or congressional inquiry, many now-confirmed conspiracies occupied the same epistemic space as those later deemed irrational. They were denied, ridiculed, or pathologized—often because acknowledging them would have required institutions to admit misconduct or abuse of power. What eventually distinguished these cases was not belief, but time.

This matters because institutions are not judged solely by what they deny, but by what history later confirms. When an institution is revealed to have coordinated deception, withheld critical information, or actively harmed those under its authority, the epistemic consequences extend far beyond the original act. Trust is not reset by exposure; it is adjusted in light of what has been revealed. Future claims are evaluated not in isolation, but against a revised baseline of credibility.

From the perspective of those who lived through such betrayals—or inherited their consequences—the lesson is not abstract. It is practical. Official denial is no longer treated as neutral. Reassurance loses its presumptive authority. What once might have been dismissed as implausible becomes, at minimum, conceivable.

This is not an argument that suspicion is always correct. It is an argument that institutions have, at times, lost the presumption of trust. When conspiracies are exposed retroactively, they alter the conditions under which future trust is extended. The public does not simply update a belief; it updates a rule: *institutional claims require verification, not deference.*

Understanding contemporary conspiracism therefore requires more than psychological explanation. It requires historical accounting. Before belief systems can be evaluated, the record of institutional behavior must be confronted—without defensiveness, without minimization, and without the assumption that skepticism itself is the pathology.

I. A Catalogue of Institutional Betrayals

The purpose of this section is not to rehearse grievance or to imply that all institutional action is deceptive. It is to establish a narrower, more difficult point: that some of the behaviors now associated with "conspiratorial thinking" were once accurate descriptions of real, coordinated misconduct—misconduct that was denied at the time, revealed later, and quietly absorbed into the historical record.

Each case presented here meets three criteria. First, the activity in question was real, documented, and confirmed through official investigation, declassification, or legal process. Second, it was initially dismissed or obscured by the institutions responsible. Third, its exposure produced lasting damage to institutional credibility that extended well beyond the immediate victims.

These cases are not presented to justify belief in any contemporary theory. They are presented to demonstrate how *epistemic expectations change*. Once deception is established as a historical fact, skepticism becomes a learned posture rather than a psychological anomaly. What follows are precedents.

COINTELPRO: Domestic Surveillance and the Criminalization of Dissent

From the mid-1950s through the early 1970s, the Federal Bureau of Investigation (FBI) operated a covert program known as COINTELPRO—short for Counter Intelligence Program— designed to surveil, infiltrate, disrupt, and discredit domestic political organizations deemed subversive. Its targets were not foreign agents or violent cells, but American citizens engaged in civil rights activism, antiwar protest, and political dissent.

The program was formally investigated and condemned by the U.S. Senate's Church Committee in the mid-1970s, which documented widespread abuse of power and constitutional violations.

Among those targeted were Martin Luther King Jr., Malcolm X, the Southern Christian Leadership Conference, the Student Nonviolent Coordinating Committee, and the Black Panther Party. Tactics included warrantless surveillance, the planting of informants, dissemination of false information to the media, encouragement of internal conflict, and efforts to destroy personal reputations. In some cases, operations were explicitly designed to provoke legal trouble, public disgrace, or organizational collapse.

At the time, allegations of such conduct were routinely denied. Critics were dismissed as paranoid, anti-government, or irresponsible. It was only after the program was exposed—first through a 1971 burglary of an FBI field office and later through congressional investigation—that the scope of the activity became undeniable.[1] The Church Committee hearings confirmed not only the existence of COINTELPRO, but the extent to which it had operated outside legal and ethical constraints.

The significance of COINTELPRO lies not only in what was done, but in how long it was denied. For years, allegations that federal authorities were deliberately disrupting domestic civil rights movements were widely dismissed as exaggerated or unfounded. In retrospect, it was an accurate description of institutional behavior.

For the communities most affected, the lesson was durable. Surveillance was no longer hypothetical. Disruption was no longer an abstraction. And official assurances of restraint no longer carried presumptive credibility. What had once sounded implausible became historically documented—altering how future claims would be received and assessed.

The Tuskegee Syphilis Study: Medical Authority and the Withholding of Care

From 1932 to 1972, the U.S. Public Health Service conducted a medical study in Macon County, Alabama, observing the progression of untreated syphilis in Black men. The participants— most of whom were poor, rural sharecroppers—were never informed of the true nature of the study. They were told they were receiving treatment for "bad blood," a vague term encompassing several ailments, and were given placebos, basic medical exams, and burial stipends as inducement to remain enrolled.

The study continued even after penicillin became a widely accepted and effective treatment for syphilis in the 1940s.[2] Rather than treat the men, researchers deliberately withheld care in order to continue observing the disease's long-term effects. Participants were actively prevented from accessing treatment elsewhere, including through military draft screenings, where intervention might otherwise have occurred.

For decades, the study operated without meaningful public scrutiny. It was not exposed through internal review or ethical oversight, but through investigative journalism in 1972, which prompted public outrage and eventual congressional inquiry.[3] By the time the program ended, dozens of men had died from syphilis or its complications, others had infected partners, and children had been born with congenital syphilis.

What distinguishes Tuskegee is not only the scale of harm, but the authority under which it was carried out. This was not a rogue experiment conducted in secret by fringe actors. It was administered by federal health officials, endorsed by medical institutions, and sustained through professional norms that prioritized data collection over human welfare. Ethical justification was supplied not by malice, but by abstraction: the belief that scientific knowledge outweighed individual consent.

The epistemic consequences were profound and enduring. For many Black Americans, Tuskegee did not register as an isolated atrocity, but as part of a longer history of medical mistreatment and racialized neglect. Public reassurances about safety, best practices, and professional ethics no longer operated on neutral ground. They were filtered through historical memory.

In this context, medical skepticism did not emerge from ignorance of science, but from experience with its misuse. Trust in public health authority was not simply lost; it was recalibrated under conditions where official guidance had once masked deliberate harm. The legacy of Tuskegee persists not because it is misunderstood, but because it is remembered.

MKUltra: Secret Experimentation and the Limits of Consent
Beginning in the early 1950s, the Central Intelligence Agency (CIA) initiated a covert research program known as MKUltra, designed to explore methods of mind control, interrogation, and psychological manipulation. Conducted under the auspices of national security during the Cold War, the program funded dozens of subprojects across universities, hospitals, prisons, and research institutions in the United States and abroad.

Many of these experiments involved the administration of psychoactive substances—most notably LSD—to unwitting subjects. In some cases, participants were prisoners, psychiatric patients, or military personnel. In others, they were ordinary citizens who had no knowledge that they were part of an intelligence experiment. Consent, when obtained at all, was often vague, misleading, or entirely absent.

For years, allegations of such activities circulated at the margins of public discourse and were routinely dismissed as speculative or fantastical. The idea that a U.S. intelligence agency would secretly drug citizens or conduct behavioral experiments without oversight sounded implausible—too extreme to be credible. That assumption did not survive exposure.

In the mid-1970s, congressional investigations revealed the existence and scope of MKUltra, confirming that the CIA had authorized and conducted experiments that violated basic ethical standards and, in some cases, resulted in lasting psychological harm. Compounding the damage, the agency had destroyed many of its own records in an effort to limit disclosure, leaving investigators to reconstruct the program from partial documentation and testimony.[4]

The significance of MKUltra lies not only in the abuses themselves, but in the institutional logic that enabled them. The program was justified internally as research, shielded externally by classification, and insulated from accountability through secrecy. Oversight mechanisms were weak or absent, and experimental objectives were often prioritized over informed consent.

For the public, the revelation recalibrated another boundary of plausibility. The idea that institutions might experiment on citizens without their knowledge was no longer the province of dystopian fiction. It had occurred, under official authority, and remained hidden for decades. As with earlier betrayals, the exposure of MKUltra did not simply add another scandal to the historical record—it altered expectations. Subsequent assurances about ethical oversight and institutional restraint were inevitably filtered through this history.

Big Tobacco, Big Pharma: Corporate Deception and the Manipulation of Risk

Throughout the twentieth century, major corporations—most prominently within the tobacco and pharmaceutical industries—

engaged in coordinated efforts to suppress, distort, or delay public understanding of the harms associated with their products. These efforts were not the result of isolated bad actors or marketing excess. They were organized, strategic, and internally documented.

In the case of tobacco, internal company records later revealed that executives understood the addictive and carcinogenic nature of cigarettes decades before this information was publicly acknowledged. Rather than disclose these findings, tobacco firms funded research designed to cast doubt on emerging scientific consensus, promoted alternative explanations for rising cancer rates, and framed the issue as one of personal choice rather than product risk. Public statements emphasized uncertainty even as private communications confirmed knowledge of harm.

For years, critics who alleged that tobacco companies were knowingly misleading the public were dismissed as alarmists or ideologues. Industry representatives insisted that the science was inconclusive and that no definitive link between smoking and disease had been established. That posture collapsed in the 1990s, when litigation forced the release of millions of internal documents and culminated in congressional testimony in which tobacco executives were compelled to confront their own records.[5]

In the opioid crisis, this pattern repeated with devastating effect, as major manufacturers, most prominently Purdue Pharma, aggressively marketed powerful painkillers as safe and non-addictive despite internal evidence of dependency risk, fueling widespread overprescription and public health collapse.[6]

A similar pattern has appeared in segments of the pharmaceutical industry, particularly in cases involving the marketing of addictive or high-risk medications. Companies promoted products as safe or non-habit forming despite internal data suggesting otherwise, while downplaying adverse effects and incentivizing overprescription through aggressive sales strategies. Regulatory oversight often lagged behind market expansion, and penalties, when imposed, were absorbed as costs of doing business rather than deterrents.

What distinguishes these cases is not only the presence of deception, but its institutional normalization. Harm was reframed as side effect, uncertainty emphasized in public communication, and accountability diffused through legal complexity.

The epistemic consequences were predictable. Once it became clear that corporations had deliberately obscured known risks while presenting themselves as trustworthy authorities, public skepticism toward official assurances expanded beyond the specific products involved. Health guidance, safety claims, and regulatory approvals began to be evaluated through a more adversarial lens. Doubt, in this context, was not a rejection of science, but a response to its manipulation.

As with earlier cases, the exposure of corporate deception altered expectations rather than resolving them. Claims of safety or responsibility could no longer rely on institutional prestige alone. They required verification, transparency, and an awareness that economic incentives might shape what was disclosed—and what was not.

Operation Northwoods: When Deception Was Formally Proposed

In 1962, senior officials within the U.S. Department of Defense drafted a set of proposals collectively known as *Operation Northwoods*, outlining plans for covert actions designed to manufacture public support for military intervention against Cuba. These plans included staging or simulating violent attacks on American civilians and military targets, which would then be attributed to the Cuban government.

The proposals were detailed, bureaucratic, and explicit. Suggested actions ranged from orchestrated acts of terrorism in U.S. cities to the fabrication of evidence implicating Cuba in the destruction of American aircraft. The objective was not defensive preparedness, but narrative control: the creation of a *casus belli*—a justification for war— through deception rather than response.

Crucially, Operation Northwoods was never implemented. The proposals were rejected by President John F. Kennedy, and no evidence suggests that the plans were carried out. But their historical significance does not depend on execution. It rests on the fact that such actions were formally conceived, documented, and advanced through the highest levels of military planning.

At the time, the notion that American officials would contemplate staging attacks on their own population would have sounded indistinguishable from extremist fantasy. It would have been dismissed as implausible, inflammatory, or unpatriotic. That judgment, like others before it, did not survive declassification.[7] When the documents were released decades later, they revealed not rogue speculation, but institutional deliberation conducted in the language of strategic necessity.

The epistemic consequence of Northwoods lies in what it made imaginable. Even in rejection, the proposals demonstrated that senior officials were willing to formally consider large-scale deception under certain strategic conditions. For the public, the lesson was not that such acts were routine, but that the boundary between protection and manipulation was thinner than official narratives had suggested.

Once again, trust was recalibrated not because an atrocity occurred, but because a previously implausible form of institutional behavior was shown to be possible—and to have been seriously entertained.

CIA Media Relationships and the Management of Narrative

Beginning in the late 1940s and expanding through the Cold War, the Central Intelligence Agency developed a covert program—later referred to as *Operation Mockingbird*—aimed at influencing domestic and foreign media coverage in ways favorable to U.S. strategic interests. The effort involved cultivating relationships with journalists, editors, and media executives, as well as providing guidance, funding, or access in exchange for cooperation.

Unlike later controversies over misinformation or propaganda, Mockingbird did not operate primarily through overt state media. Its power lay in indirection. By embedding influence within ostensibly independent news organizations, the program blurred the boundary between reporting and strategic communication. Audiences consuming the news had no way of knowing when coverage reflected editorial judgment and when it reflected intelligence priorities.

For years, claims that the intelligence community was shaping or steering mainstream media narratives were dismissed as paranoid or conspiratorial. The idea that respected journalists might function, even intermittently, as assets of the state clashed with liberal assumptions about press independence and democratic accountability.

Those assumptions were destabilized in the 1970s, when congressional investigations revealed that the CIA had maintained extensive relationships with media figures and outlets, both domestic and international. While the scope and intensity of these relationships varied, the underlying fact was confirmed: intelligence agencies had treated information not merely as something to be gathered, but as something to be managed.[8]

The epistemic damage caused by Mockingbird was subtle but lasting. Unlike overt censorship, covert influence corrodes trust invisibly. Once revealed, it does not prompt outrage alone—it produces uncertainty. If institutions tasked with informing the public can also function as instruments of persuasion, the line between knowledge and narrative becomes harder to draw.

This realization reshaped how later generations evaluated claims of media neutrality. Skepticism toward official narratives did not arise solely from ideological polarization or digital fragmentation. It was informed by historical knowledge that information ecosystems themselves had been treated as arenas of strategic manipulation. The press, once imagined as an external check on power, could also be folded into it.

Church Sexual Abuse Cover-Ups: Moral Authority and the Architecture of Silence

Over the course of the late twentieth and early twenty-first centuries, investigations across multiple countries revealed that senior leaders within major religious institutions—most prominently the Catholic Church—had systematically concealed sexual abuse committed by clergy against minors. Rather than report offenses to civil authorities, church officials often reassigned accused priests, sealed records, and prioritized institutional reputation over victim protection.

For decades, allegations of widespread abuse and coordinated cover-up were treated as isolated scandals or anti-clerical attacks. Victims were frequently disbelieved, pressured into silence, or framed as threats to the faith community. The idea that an institution dedicated to moral instruction and spiritual care could enable such harm on a systemic scale was difficult for many to accept—and easy to dismiss as exaggeration.

That dismissal collapsed under sustained investigative reporting and legal inquiry. Beginning in the early 2000s, court proceedings, grand jury reports, and journalistic investigations— most notably those examining the Archdiocese of Boston— documented patterns of concealment extending across dioceses and continents. Internal records showed that abuse was not merely tolerated but administratively managed, with knowledge of repeat offenders circulating within clerical hierarchies while remaining hidden from the public.[9]

The significance of these revelations lies not only in the crimes themselves, but in the nature of the betrayal. Unlike intelligence agencies or corporations, religious institutions derive authority not from expertise or regulation, but from moral trust. When that trust was violated—and then protected through silence—the damage extended beyond individual cases. It undermined the credibility of moral reassurance itself.

For many believers and nonbelievers alike, the exposure forced a painful recalibration. Appeals to conscience, virtue, and institutional goodness could no longer be taken at face value. The lesson absorbed was not simply that abuse had occurred, but that institutions claiming moral superiority were capable of subordinating justice to self-preservation.

This form of betrayal proved especially corrosive because it inverted expectations. Where protection was assumed, harm was hidden. Where confession was preached, secrecy prevailed. And where trust had been freely given, it was strategically exploited. In this context, skepticism toward moral authority did not reflect cynicism—it reflected recognition.

While the cases above are drawn primarily from the United States, they are not uniquely American. Comparable patterns of institutional concealment, coordinated deception, and delayed accountability have emerged across Europe and beyond, from intelligence operations to clerical abuse scandals. These dynamics are structural rather than national.

II. The Psychological Residue of Betrayal

The events catalogued above are often treated as historical facts—bounded in time, resolved through exposure, and closed by official acknowledgment. But their effects do not remain confined to the moment of revelation. They persist as *epistemic residue*: durable changes in how individuals and communities assess authority, credibility, and risk.

Betrayal, once experienced, alters expectations. When institutions are revealed to have coordinated harm, concealed knowledge, or deliberately misled the public, trust does not simply return when the truth emerges. It recalibrates. Communities learn not just *that* deception occurred, but *that it was possible*, and that it was denied until denial became untenable. The lesson absorbed is not outrage alone, but caution.

Over time, this caution becomes patterned. Communities come to expect betrayal—not in the sense of assuming constant malice, but in the sense of withholding default trust. Official assurances are no longer received as neutral starting points. They are treated as claims to be evaluated against memory. What once required evidence to doubt increasingly requires evidence to believe.

This dynamic is often misunderstood as cynicism or alienation. In practice, it functions more like inherited knowledge. Stories of surveillance, medical exploitation, or institutional silence are passed down not as abstract history, but as guidance: warnings about where vulnerability lies and how power has behaved in the past. In this way, skepticism becomes intergenerational. It is learned socially, not invented individually.

For those shaped by such histories, belief in conspiracy is not experienced as fringe or transgressive. It is experienced as continuity—a way of honoring lessons paid for at real cost. "Once lied to, forever altered" is not a slogan of paranoia, but a description of how trust, once broken by institutions, rarely returns to its original form.

This residue does not require constant reinforcement to remain active. It lies dormant until conditions resemble earlier betrayals—conflicting explanations, delayed disclosures, dismissive reassurances. When those echoes appear, past deceptions are not recalled in detail; they are activated as expectation. Suspicion, in this context, reflects a learned posture shaped by historical experience rather than a failure of reasoning.

III. Memory vs. Narrative

Exposure does not settle the meaning of betrayal. It merely opens a struggle over interpretation—one that institutions often win by controlling how history is framed, archived, and remembered. Official narratives tend to sanitize conspiratorial histories, isolating them as aberrations, procedural failures, or relics of a less enlightened past rather than as indicators of systemic vulnerability.

In this process, wrongdoing is acknowledged narrowly and contained rhetorically. Reports are released, apologies issued, and reforms promised, but the broader implications are often softened or displaced. The aim is not necessarily to deny that betrayal occurred, but to manage its significance: to ensure that it does not destabilize confidence in the institution as a whole.

Communities that retain memory rather than accept narrative closure are frequently cast as unreasonable. Continued skepticism is reframed as bitterness, paranoia, or disloyalty. To remember too much, or to insist that past behavior should inform present trust, is treated as an inability to move on—a failure of civic maturity rather than an act of prudence.

This asymmetry reveals a deeper contest: who gets to define what counts as reasonable belief. Institutions tend to reserve that authority for themselves, drawing the boundary between legitimate concern and irrational suspicion in ways that protect institutional credibility. Those who were harmed, or who learned from harm, are rarely granted equal standing in that determination.

The result is a recurring inversion. Those who point to documented betrayal are accused of undermining trust, while the behaviors that produced distrust in the first place are reclassified as closed chapters. Memory becomes a liability, and forgetting is treated as a civic virtue.

This tension between memory and narrative helps explain why official reassurances so often fail. They do not engage the substance of what was learned through betrayal; they attempt to overwrite it. In doing so, they widen rather than bridge the epistemic gap between institutions and the publics they serve.

IV. From Scandal to Structure

Taken individually, the cases outlined in this chapter are often treated as scandals—exceptional failures that reveal little beyond their immediate circumstances. Framed this way, each betrayal can be acknowledged, managed, and contained. The problem, however, is not any single incident. It is the pattern that emerges when such incidents recur across institutions, sectors, and decades.

Seen structurally, these are not isolated breakdowns but expressions of shared conditions. They reveal recurring patterns of opacity and institutional self-protection. They reflect moral drift, where institutional survival gradually displaces ethical obligation. In such conditions, elite actors face few meaningful consequences for deception or harm. They also expose the capacity of powerful institutions to shape reality through narrative control, determining not only what is disclosed, but how disclosure is interpreted.

Under these conditions, trust erodes not because people encounter one lie, but because they encounter the same logic repeatedly. Initial denial followed by exposure. Reassurance followed by revision. Formal acknowledgment often without structural reform. Over time, these sequences cease to feel accidental. They come to resemble a mode of operation.

This is the point at which conspiracy thinking shifts character. It no longer functions as a reaction to a discrete claim or event, but as an interpretive framework for understanding institutional behavior itself. Suspicion is no longer attached to one allegation; it is attached to the system that produced multiple, documented deceptions while insisting on its own credibility.

Importantly, this shift does not require assuming constant malice or coordination. It requires only the recognition that institutions operate within incentives that reward opacity, protect status, and diffuse responsibility. When those incentives remain intact across scandals, the public learns to expect recurrence. What looks from the outside like excessive suspicion often reflects an attempt to impose coherence on patterns institutions themselves refuse to name.

At this stage, disbelief is not oppositional—it is structural. It arises not from hostility toward institutions, but from observation of how they behave when challenged. Conspiracy narratives, in this light, are less about uncovering hidden plots than about making sense of recurring contradictions between institutional self-presentation and institutional conduct.

V. The Loop of Diminished Credibility

When institutional deception is formally documented, future claims are no longer evaluated in isolation. Credibility becomes cumulative: each new assertion is measured against prior exposure. Denials that might once have been persuasive now arrive burdened with history.

This dynamic creates a feedback loop. Past betrayal lowers the threshold of plausibility for future allegations, while institutional responses often fail to account for that shift. Reassurance is offered as if trust were intact, rather than as if it had been recalibrated. When those reassurances are later revised, walked back, or contradicted, the loop tightens.

In this context, skepticism becomes self-reinforcing—not because people are deluded, but because they have learned to protect themselves. Each confirmed deception functions as a reference point. "They told us that was a rumor too." "They said that couldn't have happened." These are not expressions of reflexive cynicism; they are memory cues activated by resemblance.

Institutions often misinterpret this response as bad faith. From their perspective, the public appears unwilling to accept correction, clarification, or good-faith error. What is missed is that credibility, once damaged, does not regenerate through assertion. It regenerates through behavior—and behavior is assessed cumulatively.

The loop persists because institutional incentives rarely change in response to exposure. Information is still managed, accountability remains diffuse, and consequences are often symbolic. Each new controversy is treated as an isolated communications problem rather than as evidence of a deeper trust deficit. As a result, the same patterns recur, and the public's skepticism hardens accordingly.

Over time, this dynamic produces an asymmetry. Institutions expect to be believed unless proven otherwise. The public, having learned from experience, withholds belief unless evidence is forthcoming. The gap between these expectations is where distrust takes root—and where conspiracy narratives gain traction as alternative accounts that better fit observed behavior.

Breaking this loop requires more than correction or debunking. It requires confronting the historical record that shaped the loop in the first place. Without that reckoning, institutional credibility continues to decline not because the public is irrational, but because the lessons of past betrayal remain unaddressed.

VI. Takeaway

Before belief can be judged, betrayal must be confronted. The cases examined in this chapter are not marginal episodes or historical curiosities; they are documented deceptions that reshaped the conditions under which trust is extended. Any serious account of contemporary distrust must begin here, not with speculation about irrationality or pathology.

The roots of today's skepticism lie in yesterday's record. Surveillance denied and later confirmed. Harm concealed under professional authority. Deception justified as necessity and exposed only after delay. These experiences did not disappear when they were acknowledged. They altered expectations—about honesty, accountability, and the reliability of institutional self-reporting.

To condemn belief without reckoning with this history is to mistake effect for cause. It treats suspicion as spontaneous rather than learned, as emotional rather than evidentiary. In doing so, it absolves institutions of responsibility for the epistemic environments they helped create.

Legitimate distrust does not arise from a vacuum. It is forged through encounter, reinforced by repetition, and sustained by memory. Any theory of trust that ignores this process—any appeal to credibility that bypasses accountability—rests on a fragile foundation. Trust cannot be demanded where it has been systematically undermined.

Conclusion

This chapter has argued that distrust is not merely a reaction to uncertainty, nor a byproduct of misinformation alone. It is often the rational residue of institutional behavior—earned through patterns of concealment, denial, and delayed accountability. When conspiracies are real, and when they are exposed only after resistance and ridicule, skepticism ceases to be aberrant. It becomes adaptive.

What emerges from this history is not a blanket rejection of institutions, but a conditional stance toward them. Credibility is no longer assumed; it is tested. Authority is no longer sufficient; it must be accompanied by transparency and consequence. In this sense, conspiracy belief is less a departure from reason than a response to its repeated frustration.

The question that follows is not whether institutions deserve trust in the abstract, but under what conditions they can justifiably claim it. When secrecy, withholding, or narrative control are defended as necessary, the burden of justification shifts. History alters the baseline. The issue is no longer whether institutions have the authority to manage information, but when that management becomes ethically indistinguishable from manipulation.

Chapter 4 turns to that boundary. It examines the ethics of secrecy—when withholding protects legitimate interests, and when it erodes the very credibility it is meant to preserve. The problem is not secrecy itself. It is secrecy unmoored from accountability.

REFERENCES

[1] U.S. Senate Select Committee to Study Governmental Operations with Respect to Intelligence Activities, *Final Report, Book II: Intelligence Activities and the Rights of Americans* (Washington, DC: U.S. Government Printing Office, 1976).

[2] James H. Jones, *Bad Blood: The Tuskegee Syphilis Experiment* (Free Press, 1981).

[3] Jones, *Bad Blood*; U.S. Department of Health, Education, and Welfare, *Final Report of the Tuskegee Syphilis Study Ad Hoc Advisory Panel* (Washington, DC, 1973).

[4] U.S. Senate Select Committee on Intelligence and Subcommittee on Health and Scientific Research of the Committee on Human Resources, *Project MKULTRA, the CIA's Program of Research in Behavioral Modification*, 95th Cong., 1st sess., August 3, 1977.

[5] U.S. House of Representatives, Committee on Energy and Commerce, Subcommittee on Health and the Environment, *Regulation of Tobacco Products (Nicotine Addiction)*, 103rd Cong., 2nd sess., April 14, 1994; *United States v. Philip Morris USA Inc.*, 449 F. Supp. 2d 1 (D.D.C. 2006).

[6] Patrick Radden Keefe, *Empire of Pain: The Secret History of the Sackler Dynasty* (Doubleday, 2021).

[7] Chairman, Joint Chiefs of Staff, memorandum to the Secretary of Defense, "Justification for U.S. Military Intervention in Cuba," March 13, 1962, declassified and reproduced by the National Security Archive.

[8] Carl Bernstein, "The CIA and the Media," *Rolling Stone*, October 20, 1977.

[9] Commonwealth of Massachusetts, Office of the Attorney General, *The Sexual Abuse of Children in the Roman Catholic Archdiocese of Boston* (Boston, July 23, 2003); Boston Globe Spotlight Team, "Abuse in the Catholic Church," investigative series, *Boston Globe*, beginning January 6, 2002.

Information can be withheld lawfully and still cause harm.

CHAPTER 4

The Ethics of Secrecy

When Does Institutional Withholding Become a
Form of Violence?

This chapter examines institutional secrecy not as a technical exception or administrative necessity, but as a moral practice with social consequences. Information can be withheld lawfully and still cause harm. When institutions control access to knowledge that affects people's lives, safety, or autonomy, secrecy becomes a form of power.

The central question is not whether institutions may keep secrets, but when secrecy becomes corrosive—when it undermines informed participation, shields wrongdoing, or substitutes institutional convenience for public dignity. The goal is not to reject confidentiality outright, but to distinguish necessary protection from ethically damaging silence.

I. Why Institutions Keep Secrets

Institutions justify secrecy through two overlapping but distinct logics. The first is functional: secrecy is presented as necessary to protect collective interests in complex, high-stakes environments. The second is bureaucratic: secrecy operates as a mechanism of institutional self-protection, shielding organizations and decision-makers from risk, scrutiny, and consequence. Understanding the ethics of secrecy requires separating these logics before examining how they converge.

Functional Justifications

The most commonly cited rationale for secrecy is national security. States argue that disclosing certain information would endanger lives, compromise operations, or weaken their strategic position. Similar reasoning appears in diplomatic and military contexts, where secrecy is defended as a means of preserving leverage, deterrence, or negotiation flexibility. Strategic ambiguity is treated as stabilizing rather than deceptive. It involves deliberate vagueness about capabilities, intentions, or thresholds.

In economic and technological domains, institutions invoke competitive advantage. Corporations and state agencies alike withhold information to protect intellectual property, market position, or innovation pipelines. Disclosure, in these cases, is framed as a threat not only to profitability but to long-term viability. Secrecy is thus positioned as a form of stewardship: guarding assets for the greater good of organizational continuity.

These arguments are not inherently frivolous. In certain contexts, disclosure can cause real harm. The ethical problem arises not from the existence of functional secrecy, but from its expansion—when protective logic becomes default posture and its costs remain unexamined.

Bureaucratic Incentives

Alongside these public-facing justifications operates a quieter set of incentives rooted in organizational behavior. Information is often withheld to minimize exposure—legal, professional, or reputational. Decisions made under uncertainty generate risk, and secrecy becomes a way to manage that risk by limiting who knows what, when, and on what record.

This dynamic is reinforced by bureaucratic culture. Risk aversion discourages early disclosure of incomplete or unfavorable information. Fear of liability encourages delay until responsibility can be diffused or framed defensively. Reputational concerns incentivize narrative control, particularly when mistakes, harm, or negligence may come to light. In these contexts, secrecy functions less as protection of the public and more as protection from the public.

Crucially, these incentives do not require bad faith. They emerge naturally in hierarchical institutions where accountability is uneven and consequences are asymmetric. When error carries punishment but opacity carries little cost, withholding becomes rational. Over time, secrecy normalizes not because it is always necessary, but because disclosure is perceived as personally and institutionally risky.

The Convergence Point

The ethical problem arises where functional and bureaucratic secrecy converge. Claims of national interest coexist with fear of blame; strategic ambiguity overlaps with institutional self-preservation. At this point, secrecy is no longer merely about preventing harm to others. It is increasingly about preventing harm to the institution itself.

When secrecy serves institutional protection first and public interest second, its moral status changes. Withholding becomes less a shield against harm and more a mechanism of control. It determines who assesses risk, who must defer, and who bears the consequences of ignorance. In this form, secrecy shifts power toward institutions while leaving the public more exposed to its consequences.

Recognizing this convergence is essential. The question is not whether institutions are permitted to keep secrets, but whether the reasons offered for secrecy align with its actual effects. When they do not, secrecy ceases to be a technical choice and becomes an ethical problem.

II. The Language of Withholding

Secrecy is not sustained by silence alone. It is maintained through language—through a repertoire of terms and phrases that legitimize non-disclosure while minimizing its ethical visibility. These linguistic practices do more than describe the status of information; they structure who is authorized to know, who must wait, and who is expected to defer.

A first category consists of formal euphemisms embedded in legal and administrative systems. Labels such as *classified*, *confidential*, *proprietary*, or *under active investigation* function as procedural endpoints rather than explanations. Once invoked, they foreclose further inquiry without requiring justification. The designation itself becomes the reason. Information is not withheld because disclosure would cause specific harm, but because it has been placed in a protected category whose logic is rarely interrogated.

A second category involves epistemic deflection—language that frames non-disclosure as a matter of complexity rather than power. Phrases such as *"it's too complicated for the public to understand"* or *"the data require expert interpretation"* imply that withholding is an act of responsibility. The public is positioned not as a stakeholder, but as a potential source of confusion or misinterpretation. Knowledge is treated as a technical domain best managed by credentialed insiders, even when the consequences of that knowledge fall on non-experts.

A third category relies on temporal delay. Statements like *"we're still reviewing,"* *"the science is evolving,"* or *"more information is needed"* suspend accountability without explicitly denying it. Delay is presented as prudence. Yet when used repeatedly or indefinitely, it functions as a form of quiet refusal—postponing disclosure until public attention wanes or responsibility diffuses. What appears as caution can, over time, become concealment by attrition.

Across these forms, the effect is cumulative. Language that obscures rather than explains disempowers those excluded from knowledge, while reinforcing elite gatekeeping over truth. Citizens are asked to trust not because reasons have been given, but because reasons have been linguistically deferred. The result is an epistemic hierarchy in which authority is asserted through vocabulary rather than earned through transparency.

Crucially, this language does not merely reflect secrecy; it produces it. By normalizing non-explanation, it conditions publics to accept ignorance as a procedural outcome rather than as a contested choice. In doing so, it transforms secrecy from an exceptional act into an ambient feature of institutional communication—one that distances decision-makers from those affected by their decisions.

III. When Secrecy Crosses the Ethical Line

Secrecy becomes ethically consequential not at the moment information is withheld, but at the point where withholding begins to shape outcomes. The moral question is not simply whether institutions keep secrets, but whether those secrets deny others the capacity to act with knowledge over matters that affect their lives, safety, or dignity.

The first threshold is informed decision-making. When institutions possess information about risks—environmental hazards, health threats, structural failures—and fail to disclose it, individuals are deprived of agency. They cannot consent meaningfully, protect themselves, or evaluate tradeoffs. In such cases, secrecy does not merely limit awareness; it forecloses choice. Harm arises not only from what happens, but from the removal of the ability to respond.

A second threshold is the enablement of ongoing harm. Secrecy crosses an ethical line when it allows preventable damage to continue—when toxic exposures go unacknowledged, abuse is concealed, or dangerous practices persist under the cover of non-disclosure. Here, withholding functions as a form of facilitation. Silence does not merely accompany harm; it sustains it. The ethical breach lies not in the original wrongdoing alone, but in the decision to protect the institution rather than those at risk.

A third threshold involves distortion of reality. When institutions deny, minimize, or obscure facts that contradict lived experience, secrecy becomes a form of epistemic manipulation. People are told that what they observe is incorrect, exaggerated, or misunderstood. This is not simple misinformation; it constitutes a form of epistemic distortion at scale—an attempt to impose an official version of reality that invalidates perception and undermines trust in one's own judgment.

Across these thresholds, secrecy reveals itself as active rather than passive. It is not the absence of information, but the strategic control of it. Decisions about what to disclose, when, and to whom shape the field of possible action. Those who hold knowledge govern not only outcomes, but understanding itself.

In this sense, secrecy can function as a form of violence—not always physical, but epistemic and social. It injures by constraining agency, prolonging harm, and destabilizing the capacity to distinguish truth from reassurance. When withholding reaches this point, legality offers no ethical shelter. What matters is not whether secrecy was permitted, but whether it denied others the right to know what was being done to them.

IV. Case Studies of Ethical Erosion

The ethical failures described above are not theoretical. They manifest where secrecy, delay, and narrative control intersect with real-world harm. The following cases are not exhaustive, but illustrative—each demonstrates a distinct way in which institutional withholding crossed from protection into ethical erosion.

Flint Water Crisis: Concealment and the Denial of Agency

The Flint water crisis in Flint, Michigan (2014–2016) represents a clear case in which secrecy denied affected communities the ability to make informed decisions about their own safety. State and local officials possessed early evidence that the city's water supply was contaminated with lead following a change in water source. Rather than disclose this risk promptly, officials delayed acknowledgment, questioned the validity of independent testing, and reassured residents that the water was safe.[1]

During this period, residents—many of them poor and disproportionately Black—continued to consume contaminated water, unaware of the long-term health consequences. Public complaints were dismissed as exaggerated or unscientific, and responsibility was diffused across agencies. The harm that followed was not incidental; it was enabled by withholding. Secrecy did not merely obscure information—it foreclosed the possibility of self-protection.

The ethical failure in Flint lay not only in mismanagement, but in the refusal to treat affected residents as epistemic equals. Official reassurances were prioritized over lived experience, and delay functioned as a substitute for accountability. The result was a profound collapse of trust that extended well beyond the immediate crisis.

COVID-19 Early Messaging: Delay, Minimization, and Epistemic Confusion

Early public messaging during the COVID-19 pandemic in 2020 illustrates a different form of ethical strain—one rooted less in concealment of a single fact than in shifting guidance under conditions of uncertainty. Across multiple countries, institutions initially conveyed limited risk assessments, later revised precautionary guidance, and in some cases treated dissenting hypotheses or criticisms as destabilizing to public compliance.[2]

Some of these shifts reflected genuine scientific uncertainty. Others reflected concern over panic, supply shortages, or institutional credibility. The ethical issue arises when evolving scientific understanding was not consistently accompanied by transparent explanation—when guidance shifted without clear acknowledgment of uncertainty, or when public questioning was addressed through suppression rather than substantive engagement.

Even where later scientific consensus aligned with earlier reassurances, the damage had been done. Trust eroded not because science evolved, but because institutions failed to explain *how* and *why* it was evolving. In this context, secrecy sometimes took the form of epistemic compression—simplifying or delaying information in ways that ultimately strained credibility.

This case illustrates how secrecy can operate through minimization rather than silence. When people later perceive that risks were understated or debate narrowed too quickly, subsequent corrections are often received not as clarification, but as confirmation that earlier communication was incomplete.

Punishing Whistleblowers: Loyalty to Institution vs. Loyalty to the Public

A final pattern of ethical erosion appears in the treatment of whistleblowers—individuals who disclose concealed information in the public interest and are subsequently punished by the institutions they expose. Several figures illustrate this pattern. Edward Snowden (2013) disclosed the scope of NSA surveillance programs. Reality Winner (2017) leaked classified information on foreign election interference. Frances Haugen (2021) revealed internal research on the societal harms of social media platforms. Together, these disclosures brought to light information about surveillance practices, security failures, and institutional knowledge of harm. In each case, institutions responded not by addressing the substance of the disclosure, but by criminalizing or marginalizing the discloser.[3]

The message communicated through such responses is structural: transparency is tolerated only when it is institutionally sanctioned. Unauthorized disclosure, even when factually accurate and socially consequential, is framed as betrayal. Loyalty is defined vertically—owed to the institution—rather than horizontally, toward the public affected by the withheld information.

This response mechanism reinforces secrecy by deterrence. It signals to insiders that revealing uncomfortable truths carries greater personal risk than concealing them. Over time, this dynamic cultivates silence, discourages internal correction, and ensures that secrecy persists not because it is ethically justified, but because it is enforced.

Here, secrecy becomes self-perpetuating. Institutions protect themselves not only by withholding information, but by punishing those who attempt to restore public knowledge.

V. Secrecy as Epistemic Violence

To evaluate secrecy ethically, it is necessary to name a specific kind of harm it can produce: epistemic violence. By epistemic violence, I mean the structured denial of access to knowledge that materially affects people's ability to act, consent, or protect themselves. The harm lies not simply in what is withheld, but in the institutional control of knowledge necessary for agency.

This form of harm is often invisible. It does not always announce itself as censorship or propaganda. It can operate through ordinary procedures: classification, confidentiality agreements, nondisclosure policies, proprietary claims, or bureaucratic delay. Because these mechanisms are legal and routine, they can appear morally neutral even when they are not. Epistemic violence frequently wears the appearance of professionalism.

Its consequences are also distinct. When people are deprived of reliable knowledge about risks, decisions, or exposures, the result is not only misinformation but *epistemic instability*: insecurity about what is real, confusion about what is safe, and alienation from systems that are supposed to protect them. The experience is not simply "I don't know," but "I am not allowed to know," and that difference matters. It produces dependence—on officials, on institutions, on gatekeepers—precisely where independent judgment would otherwise be possible.

Epistemic violence is most corrosive when it becomes chronic. In that condition, the public does not merely lose access to specific facts; it loses confidence that disclosure will occur before harm does. People begin to assume that truth arrives late, filtered, or only after exposure. This expectation reshapes civic life: consent becomes less meaningful, participation becomes more constrained, and trust becomes harder to sustain because knowledge itself feels managed.

The burdens of epistemic violence do not fall evenly. Those harmed are often those already marginalized: poor communities, minorities, and dissidents. These groups are more likely to be exposed to risk and less able to force disclosure. When institutions withhold information, those with fewer resources have fewer alternatives: less access to expert interpretation, fewer legal avenues, less institutional leverage, and fewer platforms from which to demand answers. The result is not only information asymmetry, but uneven exposure to its consequences.

Seen this way, secrecy is not only a question of governance or policy. It shapes the conditions under which people can assess risk, make informed decisions, and evaluate authority. When access to consequential knowledge is systematically limited, the ethical concern is not simply opacity, but the redistribution of agency that opacity produces.

VI. Institutional Rationalizations vs. Moral Consequences

When institutions defend secrecy, they often do so through a familiar set of rationalizations. Information is withheld, officials explain, for the public's own good—because disclosure might provoke panic, misunderstanding, or irresponsible behavior. In other cases, secrecy is framed as temporary and provisional: until we know more, until the investigation is complete, until the data are fully verified. In each case, withholding is presented not as control, but as restraint exercised on behalf of others.

Such arguments are not always made in bad faith. In moments of genuine uncertainty, incomplete information can cause harm if released carelessly. The ethical problem arises when these rationalizations are treated as sufficient in themselves—when they are invoked repeatedly without transparency about what is known, what is unknown, and what criteria will govern future disclosure.

At that point, the cost shifts from risk management to agency erosion. To be told that information is withheld for one's own good is to be positioned as incapable of judgment. To be told to wait indefinitely *until more is known* is to be denied a role in assessing uncertainty. These postures transform citizens from participants into dependents, expected to comply rather than to understand.

The moral consequence is not merely frustration; it is a diminishment of dignity. Democratic legitimacy rests, in part, on the assumption that people are entitled to know what affects them, even when that knowledge is incomplete or unsettling. When institutions substitute paternalism for explanation, they undermine that assumption. They treat the public less as a collective of moral agents than as an audience to be managed.

This tension is especially acute when secrecy persists after harm has occurred. Appeals to panic prevention or ongoing review ring hollow when people discover that information was withheld not to protect them, but to protect institutional standing. In those moments, reassurance retroactively becomes evidence of manipulation.

"Trust us" cannot coexist with calculated ignorance imposed from above. Trust depends on the capacity to evaluate reasons, not merely to accept conclusions. When institutions rely on paternalistic rationalizations to justify secrecy, they may preserve short-term control—but they do so at the expense of long-term legitimacy.

VII. From Secrets to Silence

Secrecy rarely operates in isolation. When withholding becomes routine, it reshapes behavior across institutional life—among insiders who learn what not to say, among potential whistleblowers who observe the costs of disclosure, among media organizations constrained by access, and among citizens accustomed to partial explanations.

Within institutions, secrecy produces anticipatory compliance. Employees learn which questions invite reprisal and which concerns are safer left undocumented. Silence becomes a professional strategy—initially defensive, eventually normative.

When disclosure is met with retaliation or prosecution, silence becomes structurally incentivized. Each punished whistleblower signals that correction carries greater personal risk than concealment. Over time, silence ceases to be exceptional and becomes expected.

Media institutions are not immune to this dynamic. Dependence on access, fear of legal entanglement, and competitive pressures can narrow the range of what is pursued or published. Stories that challenge powerful institutions may be delayed, softened, or deprioritized—not through overt censorship, but through accumulated disincentives. Silence emerges less as an individual decision than as a structural outcome.

Citizens adapt as well. When official channels repeatedly obscure or delay, participation recedes. Silence may be misread as apathy when it reflects learned futility—the belief that speaking changes little or carries risk.

Over time, silence ceases to be merely the absence of speech. It becomes complicity. Not because individuals actively endorse wrongdoing, but because a culture has formed in which non-disclosure is normalized and accountability is diffuse. In such cultures, harm can persist without clear authorship, sustained by collective restraint rather than explicit conspiracy.

A culture of silence can outlast any single falsehood. Lies invite rebuttal; silence restricts inquiry. When speaking carries risk and knowledge is conditional, ethical failure no longer depends on active deception. It persists through incentives that reward restraint over disclosure.

VIII. Takeaway

The opposite of conspiracy is not transparency. It is informed participation—the ability of people to understand what affects them, to assess risk and uncertainty, and to engage institutions as moral agents rather than passive recipients of reassurance. Transparency, when treated as a technical exercise or public-relations strategy, can coexist with profound ignorance. Participation cannot.

This chapter has argued that secrecy is not ethically neutral. When information is withheld in ways that deny agency, enable harm, or suppress the capacity to judge reality, secrecy becomes a form of power exercised over knowledge itself. Its effects are cumulative, shaping trust not through single acts of deception but through patterns of silence, delay, and managed disclosure.

Ethical governance therefore requires more than secrecy management. It demands accountability for *how* silence is used, *why* information is withheld, and *whom* that withholding ultimately serves. Institutions may retain the legal right to keep secrets, but they do not retain moral immunity when those secrets erode dignity, distort consent, or substitute paternalism for explanation.

Rebuilding trust under conditions of justified skepticism does not begin with asking the public to believe more. It begins with creating structures that allow people to know more—earlier, more honestly, and with the respect owed to those who must live with the consequences of institutional decisions.

Conclusion

Where Chapter 3 showed how betrayal recalibrates trust, this chapter has examined secrecy not as an administrative detail or legal exception, but as a moral practice with epistemic consequences. When institutions withhold information, they do more than manage risk or protect interests—they shape the conditions under which knowledge is distributed and authority is exercised. In these conditions, secrecy becomes a form of governance over understanding itself.

The central failure identified here is not the existence of secrecy, but its normalization without ethical scrutiny. Functional justifications blur into bureaucratic self-protection. Language replaces explanation. Silence outlasts accountability. Over time, these patterns erode the conditions under which trust can reasonably exist, even when no single lie can be identified.

What emerges is a paradox. Institutions rely on secrecy to preserve authority, yet the unmanaged use of secrecy undermines the very legitimacy that authority depends upon. When people learn—through experience—that truth arrives late, filtered, or only after exposure, skepticism ceases to be reactive. It becomes anticipatory. Distrust, in this sense, is not a rejection of institutions, but a response to how they have chosen to relate to the public.

This dynamic does not operate in isolation. Secrecy interacts with broader informational environments, technological systems, and media infrastructures that further complicate how knowledge is produced and evaluated. When opacity becomes ambient rather than exceptional, the boundary between necessary confidentiality and ethical harm grows increasingly difficult to discern.

The next chapter turns to that environment directly—examining how digital systems, information overload, and algorithmic mediation intensify epistemic opacity, and why, under these conditions, even well-intentioned institutions struggle to sustain credible authority.

REFERENCES

[1] Michigan Civil Rights Commission, *The Flint Water Crisis: Systemic Racism Through the Lens of Flint* (Michigan Civil Rights Commission, 2017); U.S. Environmental Protection Agency, Office of Inspector General, *Management Weaknesses Delayed Response to Flint Water Crisis* (Report No. 18-P-0221, July 19, 2018).

[2] World Health Organization, *COVID-19: Make It the Last Pandemic – Report of the Independent Panel for Pandemic Preparedness and Response* (May 2021); U.S. Centers for Disease Control and Prevention, archived COVID-19 guidance and communication materials, 2020–2021.

[3] U.S. Department of Justice, criminal complaint against Edward Snowden (2013); *United States v. Winner*, No. 1:17-cr-00034 (S.D. Ga. 2018); Frances Haugen, testimony before the U.S. Senate Committee on Commerce, Science, and Transportation, October 5, 2021.

The problem is not too little information, but abundance without orientation.

CHAPTER 5

Epistemic Opacity in the Digital Age

Information Overload, AI, and the Collapse of
Authoritative Knowledge

Concerns about truth, deception, and public understanding are not unique to the digital age. What is new is the structure of the contemporary epistemic environment. In earlier eras, constraints on public knowledge were largely conditions of scarcity: information moved slowly, circulated through visible intermediaries, and authority—however contested—was legible.

Today's challenge is different. The problem is not too little information, but abundance without orientation: access without intelligibility, mediation without accountability, and verification that is increasingly difficult for ordinary citizens to perform. This chapter introduces *epistemic opacity* to name that condition—a state in which people encounter unprecedented volumes of information while lacking stable standards for judging what is reliable, relevant, or true.

The argument is not that citizens have become more irrational, nor that misinformation alone explains modern distrust. Rather, distrust becomes rational in environments where credibility is difficult to track, institutional communication is inconsistent, and the burden of discernment is pushed downward even as epistemic power remains centralized in platforms and technical systems. The chapters that follow build on this diagnosis, showing how opacity reshapes belief, authority, and the possibilities for repair.

I. What Is Epistemic Opacity?

Epistemic opacity describes a condition in which the pathways between evidence, explanation, and credibility are no longer transparent or reliably traceable. Individuals may have access to unprecedented volumes of information, yet still lack the practical ability to determine what is accurate or trustworthy. The defining feature of this condition is not ignorance, censorship, or deception in the traditional sense, but disorientation—a breakdown in the structures that allow people to evaluate claims and situate them within a shared framework of understanding.[1]

In opaque epistemic environments, information does not arrive in coherent hierarchies. Facts circulate alongside falsehoods, expert analysis competes with performative certainty, and correction rarely displaces the narratives it seeks to amend. The problem is not simply that misinformation exists, but that the *criteria* by which information earns credibility have become unstable or contested. What matters is no longer whether information is available, but whether it can be meaningfully evaluated within a common epistemic order.[2]

It is important to distinguish epistemic opacity from secrecy. Secrecy withholds information; opacity overwhelms it. Secrecy restricts access through exclusion, classification, or silence. Opacity, by contrast, emerges through saturation, fragmentation, and mediation by systems whose internal logic is difficult or impossible for ordinary users to see. In opaque environments, individuals are not prevented from knowing; they are burdened with knowing too much, without reliable tools for discernment. Knowledge becomes abundant but unanchored.

Historically, most societies managed epistemic uncertainty through relatively stable intermediaries. Editors, professional norms, academic disciplines, regulatory institutions, and reputational hierarchies acted as filters between raw information and public understanding. These mediators were neither neutral nor just. They excluded voices, entrenched power, and—at times—systematically deceived the public. Yet they provided shared reference points for credibility. People could disagree with authorities while still recognizing where authority was located and how claims were supposed to be validated.

Epistemic opacity arises when those reference points dissolve without being replaced.[3] As traditional gatekeepers lose legitimacy and new ones operate invisibly—through algorithms, platform incentives, or technical complexity—individuals inherit epistemic responsibilities they are poorly equipped to fulfill. Citizens are asked to evaluate scientific claims, statistical models, geopolitical narratives, and technological risks independently, even as the processes that produce those claims grow more specialized and inaccessible. Responsibility migrates downward; epistemic power does not.

Epistemic opacity therefore represents a structural transformation in how knowledge functions in public life. It does not imply that truth has disappeared, nor that expertise is meaningless. It means that the social infrastructure that once translated knowledge into shared understanding has fractured. Before belief can be evaluated—or corrected—the conditions under which belief is formed must be examined. That examination begins with recognizing opacity not as a failure of citizens, but as a feature of the environments in which they are asked to judge.

II. Epistemic Scarcity Then, Epistemic Opacity Now

Earlier societies were constrained by epistemic scarcity. Information was limited, slow-moving, and unevenly distributed, often controlled by political, religious, or professional elites. Most individuals understood these limits clearly. Ignorance was explicit, and access to authoritative knowledge was visibly restricted. One might distrust institutions, resent exclusion, or challenge official accounts, but the structure of epistemic authority itself was legible. People generally knew *who* claimed the right to define truth, *how* that authority was justified, and *where* disputes were supposed to be resolved.[4]

The contemporary condition is different in kind, not merely in degree. Today's epistemic crisis does not stem from a lack of information, but from the erosion of the standards by which information becomes knowledge. Facts are abundant, yet their credibility is unstable. Expertise circulates without clear markers of validation, and authoritative claims are routinely contradicted by competing authorities with equal confidence and reach. The problem is no longer access, but the ability to determine what counts as justified belief.

This distinction matters because past ignorance is not equivalent to present confusion. In scarcity-based systems, misinformation and propaganda certainly existed, but they operated within a shared epistemic frame. Lies could be exposed because there were agreed-upon criteria for evidence, verification, and authority—even if those criteria were imperfect or unfairly applied. When deception was uncovered, it registered as a violation of an established order. Trust was breached against a known standard.[5]

In opaque environments, by contrast, standards themselves are contested or invisible. Disagreement no longer unfolds within a common framework of evaluation, but across parallel frameworks that do not recognize one another's legitimacy. Competing claims often rely on different evidentiary norms, different authorities, and different moral assumptions about who deserves trust. Under these conditions, exposure does not resolve conflict; it frequently intensifies it. What one group experiences as debunking, another experiences as narrative enforcement.

This shift explains why older models of epistemic correction increasingly fail. Traditional approaches to misinformation assume that false claims persist because people lack accurate information or sufficient explanation. The remedy, therefore, is more facts, clearer communication, or authoritative correction. But in opaque environments, the obstacle is not informational deficit. It is the absence of shared criteria for adjudication. When authority itself is disputed, correction reads as assertion, and explanation sounds like condescension.[6]

As a result, debunking often produces the opposite of its intended effect. Rather than restoring confidence, it reinforces suspicion by confirming the perception that power is attempting to close debate rather than earn credibility. This dynamic does not require bad faith on the part of institutions. It arises structurally, whenever claims of expertise are advanced without transparent standards, acknowledged limits, or visible accountability.

The transition from epistemic scarcity to epistemic opacity therefore marks a deeper transformation than the spread of false information. It signals the collapse of a shared epistemic order—the loss of agreement not about *what* is true, but about *how truth is supposed to be determined.* Earlier societies limited access to information; contemporary societies dissolve the standards by which information becomes knowledge.

Understanding this shift reframes the contemporary crisis of trust. It suggests that disbelief is not primarily a rejection of facts, but a response to environments in which facts no longer arrive with reliable warrants. Until the criteria of authority are made legible again, appeals to accuracy alone will continue to fail—because what is in question is not content, but credibility itself.

III. From Broadcast Authority to Algorithmic Mediation

The transition from broadcast media to digital platforms fundamentally altered how credibility is organized in public life.

Under broadcast conditions, information flowed through centralized institutions—newspapers, radio, television networks, and professional journals—that exercised visible gatekeeping power. Editors, producers, and institutional norms filtered claims before they reached the public. Trust in these institutions was often contested and, at times, badly misplaced, but it was at least intelligible. Audiences generally knew where claims came from, who was responsible for them, and where accountability was supposed to lie.[7]

This system imposed clear epistemic hierarchies, providing a shared framework for credibility. Disputes unfolded within recognizable boundaries: facts could be challenged, authorities questioned, and narratives exposed precisely because the rules governing legitimacy were broadly understood. Even when institutions failed, they failed within a legible epistemic order.

Digital platforms replaced this structure with algorithmic mediation. Content is no longer curated primarily through editorial judgment or professional standards, but through automated systems optimized for engagement—clicks, shares, watch time, and emotional resonance. Algorithms decide what is surfaced, repeated, and amplified, yet the criteria governing those decisions remain largely opaque to users.[8] What appears as organic relevance is often the product of invisible optimization processes that privilege attention over verification.

As a result, credibility becomes detached from provenance. Claims circulate not because they have passed through recognized standards of validation, but because they perform well within platform incentive structures. Visibility substitutes for authority; repetition substitutes for confirmation. The question "Who vetted this?" gives way to "Why am I seeing this?"—a question few users can meaningfully answer.

The epistemic consequence is fragmentation. Individuals encounter different facts, narratives, and emphases depending on behavioral signals they do not fully perceive and cannot easily control. Two people following the same event may receive entirely different informational landscapes, each internally coherent, each reinforced by repetition, and each insulated from contradiction.[9] Shared reality weakens not because truth disappears, but because exposure diverges.

This fragmentation is an emergent property of systems designed to maximize relevance rather than reliability. Algorithms learn what captures attention, not what sustains understanding. Over time, they sort audiences into increasingly distinct informational environments, narrowing exposure while intensifying confidence. What feels like personalization from the user's perspective functions, epistemically, as partition.

In such environments, disagreement shifts character. It becomes less about weighing evidence within a shared frame and more about competing realities that do not recognize one another's standards of credibility. Appeals to common facts lose traction because the conditions that once produced common facts have eroded. Authority no longer fails visibly; it dissolves into a plurality of signals without clear hierarchy. The consequence of this shift is structural. When credibility is no longer anchored in transparent processes or accountable institutions, trust cannot stabilize. People are left to infer reliability from popularity, affect, or alignment with prior belief. Under algorithmic mediation, epistemic judgment is individualized while epistemic power remains centralized. It is embedded in systems whose operation is largely inaccessible to those subject to their effects.

This transformation does not merely complicate public knowledge. It alters the very grammar of belief. When individuals inhabit informational worlds that feel complete yet irreconcilable, skepticism toward external claims becomes rational rather than pathological. Distrust, in this context, is not a rejection of evidence, but a response to environments in which evidence no longer arrives with shared warrants.

IV. The AI Effect: Plausibility Without Provenance

Artificial intelligence intensifies epistemic opacity by further weakening the connection between content and origin. Generative systems can now produce text, images, audio, and video that are indistinguishable from authentic human output. As a result, provenance becomes a technical problem—solvable only through infrastructure (watermarking, authentication, chain-of-custody systems) that most users cannot access or independently audit. As these systems proliferate across information ecosystems, the central epistemic question subtly shifts—from *"Is this true?"* to *"Does this seem real enough to believe?"* That shift marks a profound change in how credibility is assessed.

This matters because plausibility is not truth. AI-generated content can be coherent, fluent, and emotionally compelling while remaining detached from any verifiable source or accountable author. Traditional cues of credibility—professional presentation, technical fluency, narrative polish—lose much of their signaling value when they can be produced at scale by systems indifferent to accuracy.[10] What once signaled expertise now often signals only stylistic competence.

The erosion of provenance is especially consequential. In earlier epistemic orders, even false or misleading claims typically originated from identifiable actors: institutions, publishers, experts, or ideologues who could, at least in principle, be interrogated, corrected, or held responsible. Generative AI introduces content that is origin-agnostic by design. Attribution becomes ambiguous, authorship diffuse, and intent difficult to infer. When content circulates without a clear source, accountability dissolves alongside it.[11]

Institutions have struggled to respond to this transformation. Verification mechanisms lag behind production capabilities, and existing safeguards are poorly suited to environments in which fabrication is cheap, rapid, and increasingly undetectable. Official responses often emphasize caution—warnings about deepfakes, misinformation, or synthetic media—without providing citizens with usable tools for judgment. People are told to be skeptical, but not how to verify; warned about manipulation, but not given stable anchors of trust.

This response gap compounds epistemic fatigue. When individuals are repeatedly cautioned that content may be deceptive, yet offered no reliable means of authentication, skepticism hardens into disengagement. The burden of discernment is placed on the individual precisely as discernment becomes most difficult. What appears as epistemic empowerment is experienced, in practice, as abandonment.[12]

Under these conditions, trust erodes not because people reject expertise, but because expertise no longer appears accessible. Systems that generate and circulate knowledge become too complex to understand, audit, or meaningfully contest. Authority feels abstract and unaccountable—located somewhere within technical infrastructures rather than embodied in identifiable institutions or persons. When explanation gives way to automated output, and correction lags behind circulation, epistemic opacity deepens.

The significance of AI is not only its capacity to produce falsehoods, but its ability to destabilize the relationship between appearance and justification. In environments saturated with plausible but ungrounded content, belief becomes increasingly detached from verification. Judgment shifts from evidentiary assessment to affective resonance. What feels convincing travels faster than what can be confirmed. In such conditions, distrust is not a refusal of reason; it is a rational response to a world in which the signals of reason have been systematically scrambled.

V. Institutional Self-Sabotage and the Gaslighting Effect

Epistemic opacity is compounded when institutions undermine their own credibility through inconsistent communication. Reversals, contradictions, and premature certainty—especially when paired with dismissive or punitive responses to dissent— teach the public that official narratives are provisional at best and manipulative at worst. Trust erodes not simply because institutions are wrong, but because they appear unwilling to acknowledge uncertainty, error, or the limits of their own knowledge.[13]

Recent patterns of institutional communication illustrate this dynamic repeatedly. Claims initially dismissed as illegitimate have, in some cases, later been reframed by institutions themselves as plausible, incomplete, or in need of further investigation. Guidance framed as settled science has been revised without clear explanation of why earlier certainty was warranted, or why revision should now be trusted. In these cases, the core problem is not correction itself. Knowledge evolves. The problem lies in how correction is handled—whether uncertainty is admitted early, revision explained transparently, and dissent treated as inquiry rather than threat.

When institutions deny uncertainty, suppress debate, or conflate disagreement with bad faith, they generate what can be described as a form of institutional gaslighting at scale. Individuals are told that their questions are illegitimate, irresponsible, or dangerous, only to discover later that those questions were reasonable or even necessary. The lesson absorbed is not that institutions learn and adapt, but that they posture—asserting authority when confident, retreating without accountability when proven wrong.[14]

This dynamic is especially corrosive because it targets epistemic agency itself. People are not merely misinformed; they are taught to distrust their own judgment. Lived experience, inference, and provisional skepticism are dismissed in favor of official reassurance—until reassurance is quietly withdrawn. Over time, this produces learned disbelief.[15] Citizens do not conclude that every institutional claim is false; they conclude that institutional confidence is unreliable.

Once this pattern is established, even accurate information struggles to persuade. Prior behavior becomes a heuristic—a mental shortcut for judging credibility under uncertainty. "They lied before" functions not as a literal accusation applied to every statement, but as an expectation about how institutions behave under pressure. Credibility erodes cumulatively, not episodically. Each subsequent correction arrives already burdened by memory.

Importantly, this erosion does not require conspiracy, malice, or coordinated deception. It can arise from incentives that reward

74

certainty over humility, message discipline over explanation, and reputational protection over epistemic honesty. Yet the epistemic consequences are the same. When institutions prioritize authority maintenance over truthfulness about uncertainty, they sabotage the very trust they seek to preserve.

In such environments, distrust becomes anticipatory rather than reactive. Skepticism is no longer triggered by a specific claim, but by the institutional posture surrounding claims. What people reject is not expertise itself, but the performance of expertise divorced from accountability. Under conditions of repeated self-sabotage, distrust becomes a rational response to how authority presents itself—less a rejection of expertise than a judgment about its credibility.

VI. Misinformation Is Not the Primary Problem

Public discourse often frames contemporary mistrust as a misinformation crisis. False content, in this view, spreads because citizens are misled, insufficiently educated, or cognitively vulnerable. While misinformation is real and consequential, this framing misidentifies the primary source of epistemic breakdown. Most citizens are not committed conspiracists or ideological extremists. They are fatigued truth-seekers navigating environments that demand constant evaluation while offering no stable criteria for judgment.

The defining condition is not deception alone, but epistemic fatigue—a state produced when individuals are repeatedly asked to perform complex acts of verification without the tools, time, or shared standards necessary to do so. People are expected to vet technical claims across unfamiliar domains, track continual revisions in expert guidance, and decide whom to trust in the absence of agreed-upon authorities. The cumulative burden of these demands transforms truth-seeking from a civic activity into a cognitive ordeal.[16]

This fatigue is not a failure of motivation or intelligence. It is a rational response to environments in which epistemic labor has been privatized. Individuals are asked to adjudicate disputes among experts, institutions, and media systems that themselves appear divided, defensive, or opaque.[17] Under these conditions, verification becomes both necessary and impossible. People adapt by conserving cognitive resources. They disengage selectively, simplify judgments, or rely on heuristics—mental shortcuts that make uncertainty more manageable.

In such environments, narrative coherence begins to compete successfully with evidentiary rigor. Explanations that offer clear causality, moral clarity, and emotional resolution become attractive not because they are necessarily accurate, but because they restore a sense of orientation. These narratives reduce the cognitive and emotional toll of uncertainty. They answer questions decisively in contexts where official explanations remain provisional, abstract, or perpetually revised.

Importantly, this turn toward simplification should not be read as hostility toward truth. It reflects the rising cost of pursuing it. When truth requires sustained vigilance, technical literacy, and continuous reassessment—without reciprocal transparency from institutions—many people conclude that the effort exceeds the reward. What emerges is not gullibility, but triage: a pragmatic narrowing of attention in response to epistemic overload.

This perspective reframes the role of misinformation. False claims do not succeed merely because they deceive, but because they economize on doubt. They reduce complexity, resolve ambiguity, and assign responsibility in ways that institutional communication often avoids.[18] In doing so, they exploit—not create—the conditions of fatigue. Treating misinformation as the root problem therefore risks addressing the symptom while leaving the underlying epistemic environment intact.

Understanding mistrust this way shifts attention from "bad content" to epistemic conditions—the ways people come to know what is true. When verification becomes a privatized burden and authority remains disputed, citizens adapt by relying on shortcuts that reduce uncertainty at manageable cost. The next section explains why those shortcuts are not merely personal habits but incentivized outcomes of platform design.

VII. Platform Incentives and Narrative Distortion

Digital platforms are not epistemically neutral environments. Their core incentive structures reward engagement rather than accuracy, visibility rather than verification. Content that provokes outrage, certainty, or fear reliably travels farther than content that explains complexity, uncertainty, or tradeoffs. Over time, this incentive architecture reshapes public epistemology—not by dictating what people believe, but by privileging *which forms of belief are most likely to circulate*.[19]

Narratives that are simple, adversarial, and morally charged outperform those that are nuanced or provisional. Clear villains outperform structural explanations. Decisive claims outperform conditional ones. Confidence, especially when expressed emotionally, signals credibility more effectively than caution or restraint. As a result, truth competes at a systematic disadvantage against stories that *feel* true[20]—stories that provide coherence, urgency, and moral orientation without demanding sustained cognitive effort.

This dynamic reflects the ordinary functioning of platforms optimized for attention. Algorithms learn from engagement signals, not epistemic quality. They amplify what keeps users watching, clicking, and sharing, regardless of whether the underlying claims are accurate, incomplete, or misleading. Over time, this produces a selective environment in which emotionally resonant narratives are reinforced through repetition, while deliberative or uncertain explanations struggle to gain traction.

The epistemic consequence is distortion rather than falsehood alone—the reshaping of how information is interpreted, not just whether it is true or false. Even accurate information, when framed cautiously or contextually, appears weak in comparison to confident misrepresentation. Nuance is interpreted as evasion; revision as incompetence; uncertainty as unreliability. The very virtues of responsible knowledge production—provisionality, self-correction, acknowledgment of limits—become liabilities in systems that reward immediacy and conviction.

As these patterns normalize, public expectations shift. People learn, often implicitly, that persuasive communication looks decisive, moralized, and emotionally charged.[21] Institutional communication that resists these forms in favor of careful explanation appears out of step, while communication that adopts them risks sacrificing epistemic integrity. Either way, credibility suffers. What platforms reward and what epistemic responsibility requires increasingly diverge.

The result is an environment in which distortion consistently outperforms deliberation. This does not mean that truth disappears, but that it circulates under adverse conditions. When the pathways of visibility are aligned against epistemic restraint, belief formation becomes skewed toward narratives that simplify, polarize, and moralize. In such contexts, mistrust does not emerge because people reject evidence, but because evidence is consistently outperformed by more compelling alternatives.

Understanding this incentive structure is critical. Without it, epistemic breakdown is misattributed to individual irrationality or malicious actors alone. With it, distortion appears as a predictable outcome of systems that monetize attention while externalizing epistemic cost. The problem is not simply what platforms allow, but what they reliably reward. When public attention is trained to treat confidence as credibility and immediacy as proof, institutions face a lose–lose choice. They can adapt to the platform grammar and cheapen epistemic integrity, or resist it and appear evasive, weak, or out of touch. Either way, the result is the same: authority becomes harder to recognize as authority.

VIII. The Collapse of Authoritative Knowledge

For much of modern public life, authority derived not from infallibility, but from visible processes of verification. Peer review, editorial oversight, and institutional accountability provided recognizable pathways through which claims earned legitimacy.

These processes were imperfect and often exclusionary, but they made authority legible.

In opaque environments, that legibility breaks down. Claims arrive without visible warrants, disagreement lacks a common court of appeal, and correction no longer restores confidence because the legitimacy of the correcting institution is itself contested.

This transformation helps explain why trust in experts has declined even as reliance on knowledge persists. Most people have not abandoned the idea that expertise matters. What they increasingly doubt is whether experts remain accountable, responsive, or oriented toward public understanding. When expertise appears shielded from consequence, insulated from lived experience, or inconsistent in explanation, its authority weakens— not because it is wrong, but because it is no longer *recognizable* as authoritative.

The problem is compounded when expert communication relies heavily on abstraction. Statistical models, probabilistic language, and technical reassurances may be epistemically appropriate, yet experientially alienating when people are confronting concrete harm, risk, or uncertainty. When explanations fail to acknowledge this gap—when they substitute procedural correctness for moral or experiential recognition—credibility erodes.[22] Authority comes to feel detached rather than earned.

The collapse of authoritative knowledge does not eliminate truth; it disrupts the shared infrastructure that once made truth publicly recognizable. In such conditions, disagreement no longer resolves through shared standards. Competing claims are evaluated within distinct interpretive communities, each with its own criteria of authority. What breaks down is not debate itself, but the possibility of settling it.[23]

This collapse marks a decisive shift in the epistemic foundations of public life. Authority does not disappear; it loses its capacity to command trust beyond its own institutional boundaries.

Understanding this distinction is critical. The crisis of trust is not a rejection of reason, but a failure of epistemic governance— the erosion of the institutions, practices, and expectations that once made authority recognizable as legitimate. Until those structures are repaired, efforts to restore trust through assertion, expertise, or correction alone will continue to falter.

IX. The New Epistemic Landscape

The contemporary epistemic environment is no longer organized around shared standards of verification or commonly recognized authorities. Instead, it is characterized by competing truths without common adjudicators, filtered realities shaped by invisible systems, and persistent uncertainty without acknowledged limits. People are surrounded by explanations, yet increasingly unsure how to evaluate them.

In the absence of common arbiters, disagreement ceases to function as a productive epistemic process. Conflicting claims are no longer weighed within a shared framework of evidence or procedure, but asserted from within parallel interpretive worlds. What counts as proof, credibility, or expertise varies across communities, platforms, and identities.[24] As a result, disagreement often hardens rather than resolves, because it is no longer clear what resolution would even mean.

This fragmentation is intensified by mediation systems that filter reality without revealing their logic. Algorithmic curation shapes exposure while concealing its criteria, producing informational environments that feel organic and self-evident from the inside. Individuals experience their informational world as representative of reality itself, while remaining largely unaware of how that world has been constructed. The result is not simply bias, but epistemic enclosure—a condition in which reality appears coherent locally while diverging globally.[25]

At the same time, uncertainty becomes ambient rather than bounded. Institutions continue to speak with confidence while revising claims, delaying disclosure, or qualifying responsibility after the fact. Yet uncertainty is rarely acknowledged as such. Instead of being named, contextualized, and managed transparently, it is deferred, minimized, or rhetorically smoothed over. This produces a paradoxical condition in which people are told both that matters are settled and that they must remain adaptable—without being told where the limits of knowledge actually lie.

Within this landscape, conspiracy narratives gain appeal not because they are more accurate, but because they are more adjudicable. They supply identifiable agents, stable motives, and clean causal lines. Institutional explanations, by contrast, feel abstract and contingent, and responsibility remains diffuse. Opacity is reinterpreted as design; uncertainty is reinterpreted as concealment.[26]

Belief, under these conditions, becomes a means of regaining orientation. It offers cognitive closure where official narratives remain open-ended, and moral clarity where responsibility appears diffuse. This does not mean that conspiratorial belief is epistemically justified. It means that it is epistemically responsive— adapted to environments in which coherence is scarce and accountability feels inaccessible.

Seen in this light, conspiracism is not best understood as a rejection of reality, but as an attempt to survive its incoherence. It functions as an alternative epistemic order, one that trades evidentiary rigor for narrative completeness and explanatory restraint for moral certainty. Its appeal lies not in its truthfulness, but in its capacity to make a fragmented world feel intelligible.

This landscape poses a profound challenge for democratic societies. When people can no longer agree on how knowledge becomes authoritative, persuasion falters, correction fails, and trust becomes increasingly difficult to rebuild. The task that follows is not merely to counter false claims, but to reconstruct the epistemic conditions under which shared judgment is once again possible.

Conclusion

In the age of epistemic opacity, distrust is not a cognitive failure. It is an adaptive response to environments that no longer support reliable judgment. When truth becomes difficult to verify and authority difficult to interpret, skepticism functions less as rebellion than as self-defense. Doubt emerges not because people reject reason, but because the conditions that once made reason actionable have eroded.

This chapter has argued that modern conspiracism cannot be understood without accounting for the informational systems that shape belief. Algorithmic mediation, institutional inconsistency, artificial plausibility, and the collapse of shared epistemic standards together create environments in which verification is burdensome, authority is unstable, and explanation is routinely displaced by assertion. Under such conditions, mistrust is not anomalous. It is learned.

The implications extend beyond any single society or media system. Epistemic opacity is not a localized malfunction but a structural feature of modern information environments wherever institutional authority collides with fragmentation and declining legitimacy.

The next chapter turns inward to the structural logic that sustains perceptions of hidden power. A brief interlude then pauses to reflect on how these dynamics are experienced and interpreted, before the analysis widens again in Chapter 7 to the comparative and institutional contexts in which mistrust takes distinct political forms.

REFERENCES

[1] Building on Paul Humphreys, *Extending Ourselves: Computational Science, Empiricism, and Scientific Method* (Oxford University Press, 2004).

[2] Herbert A. Simon, "Designing Organizations for an Information-Rich World," in *Computers, Communications, and the Public Interest*, ed. Martin Greenberger (Johns Hopkins University Press, 1971); Neil Postman, *Amusing Ourselves to Death: Public Discourse in the Age of Show Business* (Penguin Books, 1985).

[3] Onora O'Neill, *A Question of Trust* (Cambridge University Press, 2002).

[4] Jürgen Habermas, *The Structural Transformation of the Public Sphere* (MIT Press, 1989).

[5] O'Neill, *A Question of Trust*.

[6] Quassim Cassam, *Conspiracy Theories* (Polity Press, 2019).

[7] Habermas, *The Structural Transformation of the Public Sphere*.

[8] Shoshana Zuboff, *The Age of Surveillance Capitalism* (PublicAffairs, 2019).

[9] Yochai Benkler, Robert Faris, and Hal Roberts, *Network Propaganda: Manipulation, Disinformation, and Radicalization in American Politics* (Oxford University Press, 2018).

[10] Humphreys, *Extending Ourselves*.

[11] Luciano Floridi, *The Ethics of Information* (Oxford University Press, 2013).

[12] O'Neill, *A Question of Trust*.

[13] O'Neill, *A Question of Trust*.

[14] Cassam, *Conspiracy Theories*; Stephan Lewandowsky, Ullrich K. H. Ecker, Colleen M. Seifert, Norbert Schwarz, and John Cook, "Misinformation and Its Correction: Continued Influence and Successful Debiasing," *Psychological Science in the Public Interest* 13, no. 3 (2012).

[15] Miranda Fricker, *Epistemic Injustice: Power and the Ethics of Knowing* (Oxford University Press, 2007).

[16] Simon, "Designing Organizations for an Information-Rich World."

[17] O'Neill, *A Question of Trust*.

[18] Mark Fenster, *Conspiracy Theories: Secrecy and Power in American Culture* (University of Minnesota Press, 2008); Hugo Mercier and Dan Sperber, *The Enigma of Reason* (Harvard University Press, 2017).

[19] Zuboff, *The Age of Surveillance Capitalism*.

[20] Soroush Vosoughi, Deb Roy, and Sinan Aral, "The Spread of True and False News Online," *Science* 359, no. 6380 (2018).

[21] Tarleton Gillespie, *Custodians of the Internet* (Yale University Press, 2018); Cass R. Sunstein, *#Republic: Divided Democracy in the Age of Social Media* (Princeton University Press, 2017).

[22] Niklas Luhmann, *Trust and Power* (Chichester: Wiley, 1979).

[23] Jürgen Habermas, *Between Facts and Norms* (MIT Press, 1996).

[24] Peter L. Berger and Thomas Luckmann, *The Social Construction of Reality* (Anchor Books, 1966).

[25] Gillespie, *Custodians of the Internet*.

[26] Fenster, *Conspiracy Theories: Secrecy and Power in American Culture*.

People reach for the term 'deep state' when they sense that power does not leave.

CHAPTER 6

Shadows That Stay

The Structural Logic Behind Deep State Belief

Few political phrases carry as much ridicule and emotional charge as "the deep state." To critics, it evokes fantasies of secret rooms, shadowy cabals, and unseen hands pulling the strings of history. To believers, it names something simpler and unsettling: the sense that power does not leave when politicians do.

It is tempting to dismiss deep state rhetoric as paranoid excess—and in some cases, it may be. But dismissal alone cannot explain why the belief persists across elections, across parties, and across vastly different political moments. Nor can it explain why the idea resonates even among citizens who reject its more elaborate conspiratorial claims. The phrase continues to feel descriptively accurate, even when its imagery is not.

This chapter begins from that tension. It treats "deep state" belief not as a literal account of hidden coordination, but as experiential shorthand—a way of naming the feeling that parts of the system appear insulated from democratic change, unanswerable to public scrutiny, and immune to consequence. The myth is often crude. The intuition it expresses is not.

The focus here is not on whether a secret cabal exists. It is on why so many people experience the modern state as continuous without consent. Long-standing institutions are designed to provide stability, expertise, and continuity. But when continuity becomes untouchability—when authority persists without explanation, correction, or visible accountability—it begins to feel illegitimate, regardless of intent.

Understanding this distinction matters. If "deep state" belief is treated only as irrational paranoia, the conditions that give rise to it remain unexamined. If it is treated as literal truth, it collapses into accusation without analysis. Here, we ask what people are *responding to* when they reach for this language, and what that response reveals about how power is now experienced.

What follows does not offer a theory of conspiracism, a taxonomy of belief, or a program of reform. Rather, it offers a diagnosis. By isolating the structural and experiential sources of deep state belief, this chapter prepares the ground for the comparative analysis that follows—where similar dynamics appear in different political systems under different moral and institutional conditions.

I. The Myth and the Mirror

When people talk about the "deep state," they rarely do so in analytical terms. The phrase surfaces in fragments—half-jokes, accusations, overheard remarks, and online shorthand. It is invoked to explain why nothing seems to change, why certain decisions feel inevitable, or why elections appear to alter tone but not trajectory. The language is imprecise, often exaggerated, and frequently dismissed before it is understood.

At its most extreme, the imagery is theatrical: secret rooms, coordinated elites, shadowy figures pulling levers behind the scenes. These images invite ridicule, and for good reason. They suggest a level of coherence and intentionality that rarely exists in complex systems. They flatten institutional reality into a single hidden will and convert frustration into suspicion.

But beneath this imagery lies a simpler and more persistent perception. People reach for the term "deep state" when they sense that power does not leave. Leaders come and go, but policies persist. Promises are made, votes are cast, and yet familiar outcomes reappear with remarkable consistency. The feeling is not that something is hidden, but that something remains in place regardless of who is in office.

This is the mirror embedded in the myth: the phrase reflects back an experience rather than describing a hidden reality. It gives shape to the experience of watching authority outlast accountability. What is being named is not a secret conspiracy, but a continuity that feels untouched by public will. The imagery may be fantastical, but the perception it encodes is grounded in everyday observation.

For many, the belief does not arise from exposure to fringe narratives or hidden documents. It emerges from repetition. The same explanations, the same constraints, the same limits are offered again and again, even as circumstances change. Over time, this repetition hardens into a sense that outcomes are predetermined, that power operates on a different timeline than democratic choice.

The mistake is to treat the imagery as the claim. When that happens, the intuition behind it is lost. The myth becomes an object of mockery, and the experience that produced it goes unnamed. Yet it is precisely that experience—the sense of durable authority without visible turnover—that sustains the belief long after its most elaborate versions have been rejected.

The myth is wrong in form. The experience it expresses remains. What follows traces how that feeling emerges from structures designed for stability, and why stability, when unaccompanied by visible responsiveness, is so easily mistaken for illegitimacy.

II. Continuity Without Consent

Modern democratic systems are built to balance two competing demands: responsiveness to public will and continuity of governance. Elections are meant to produce change, but not rupture. Institutions are designed to outlast individual leaders, preserve expertise, and maintain operational stability across political cycles. In principle, this balance allows democratic choice to coexist with administrative competence.

In practice, however, continuity can feel like permanence beyond reach.

From the perspective of those outside the machinery of government, the distinction between stability and permanence is not always visible. Policies remain in place despite electoral turnover. Strategic priorities shift in language but not in outcome. Crises prompt new rhetoric while familiar institutional responses reassert themselves. Over time, the system appears less adaptive than advertised, and less responsive than promised.

This perception is reinforced by the language institutions use to describe themselves. Terms such as "career staff," "institutional memory," and "inter-agency consensus" are meant to signal professionalism and continuity. Internally, they refer to expertise accumulated over time and coordination across complex organizations. Externally, they can sound very different. To citizens, this language often translates as insulation: a reminder that the people who implement and sustain policy were not elected, are rarely replaced, and are largely unaffected by shifts in public mood.

The result is a widening gap between democratic turnover and institutional persistence. Voters may replace representatives, but the underlying structures that shape policy execution remain largely intact. This requires no secrecy, coordination, or intent. It is a function of scale, specialization, and bureaucratic design.

Political scientist Michael Glennon has described this condition as a form of "double government," in which elected officials appear to govern while real continuity resides within entrenched administrative and security institutions.[1] The point is not that these actors conspire, but that they constrain. They set boundaries around what is feasible, redirect initiatives through procedural channels, and outlast reform efforts through endurance rather than resistance.

From within the system, this continuity appears necessary. From outside it, the same continuity can feel unchosen. Authority persists without visible renewal, and constraint appears without clear consent. Decisions may be lawful, procedurally correct, and professionally justified, yet still experienced as disconnected from democratic intent.

This is where perceptions of a "deep state" begin to take shape—not as claims of hidden coordination, but as responses to durable power that seems to operate independently of electoral cycles. The system does not feel covert. It feels permanent. And permanence, when it is not accompanied by visible accountability or explanation, is easily mistaken for illegitimacy.

What emerges here is not a conspiracy, but a structural condition: durability without consent. Power continues, not because it is secretly protected, but because it is institutionally embedded. For many citizens, this distinction makes little difference in lived experience. What matters is not whether authority is designed to persist, but whether that persistence remains meaningfully connected to public choice.

III. Folk Theories of Power

When formal explanations fail to resonate, people construct informal ones. These explanations are rarely systematic, often imprecise, and frequently dismissed by experts. Yet they perform an important function. They allow individuals to make sense of forces that affect their lives but remain difficult to observe, describe, or influence. In this sense, "deep state" belief operates as a folk theory of power.

Folk theories are not technical accounts. They are informal, incomplete, and rooted in experience. They emerge when official language feels disconnected from lived reality—when the words used to describe governance do not match how governance is felt. People reach for metaphors, shortcuts, and emotionally legible narratives to fill the gap left by abstraction.

The triggers for these folk theories are not obscure. Policies appear unchanged across administrations. Intelligence failures produce few visible consequences. Whistleblowers are punished while officials who mislead face little sanction. Military actions unfold with minimal public debate and are later acknowledged only after their effects are irreversible. None of these patterns require secrecy to be noticed. They are encountered through repetition.

Most citizens do not possess, nor should they be expected to possess, a technical vocabulary for institutional drift, bureaucratic inertia, or regulatory capture. They do not speak in terms of administrative continuity, path dependence, or organizational self-preservation. What they experience instead is a mismatch between democratic expectation and institutional behavior. The language available to name that mismatch is limited.

"Deep state" fills that gap. It compresses a diffuse set of observations into a single, intuitive explanation. It offers a way to say: *something is operating beyond reach*. As an account of how power actually functions, it is often wrong in detail. It exaggerates coherence, imputes intent where structure is sufficient, and personalizes systems that are better understood as processes.

But as a diagnosis of experience, it is frequently accurate. It names the sensation of being governed by forces that do not respond visibly to participation, consent, or dissent. It expresses frustration with durability that feels immune to pressure and authority that appears detached from consequence.

The mistake is to evaluate folk theories only on their factual precision. Doing so obscures the conditions that made them plausible in the first place. Incorrect details do not necessarily imply a misdiagnosis. When institutional language fails to explain continuity, exclusion, or insulation, informal narratives step in to supply meaning. Until those underlying conditions are addressed, or at least named, folk theories will continue to feel more truthful than official accounts, regardless of their inaccuracies.

IV. Populism and the Weaponization of Distrust

Belief in a "deep state" does not remain politically neutral for long. Once the intuition of unaccountable continuity takes hold, it becomes available for strategic use. Populist leaders are often the first to recognize this opportunity. They do not invent the feeling that power is distant or insulated; they give it a face, a voice, and a target.

The core move is translation: structural alienation is personalized. Durable institutions become enemies. Procedural constraint is recast as intentional obstruction. What was once a diffuse sense of exclusion is sharpened into a story of betrayal, in which opposition is no longer merely political but conspiratorial from within. The system is not just flawed; it is portrayed as actively working against "the people."

This move is powerful precisely because it builds on something real. Populist rhetoric gains traction not by creating distrust from nothing, but by amplifying existing estrangement. Where institutions already feel opaque, insulated, or immune to consequence, claims of internal sabotage resonate more easily. The narrative does not need to be accurate in detail to feel convincing in effect.

In this process, distrust is no longer a response to experience. It becomes an instrument. Leaders position themselves as the sole interpreters of hidden truth, the only figures willing to confront unseen forces. Structural limits on power—oversight, courts, independent agencies—are reframed as evidence of conspiracy rather than as features of governance. Accountability mechanisms are no longer safeguards; they are portrayed as weapons used by hostile elites.

The consequence is a shift in how institutions are perceived. Instead of being evaluated for performance, transparency, or responsiveness, they are judged by presumed allegiance. Legitimacy erodes not through demonstrated failure alone, but through narrative capture. Once institutions are recast as enemies by definition, no explanation they offer can be taken at face value. Accountability itself is reinterpreted as sabotage.

This is how distrust becomes weaponized. What began as a vernacular attempt to name unresponsive power is redirected into a political strategy that thrives on permanent suspicion. The underlying estrangement is not addressed; it is intensified. Distrust is no longer a signal of misalignment—it is a tool for mobilization.

Understanding this distinction matters. To critique populist exploitation without acknowledging the conditions that make it effective is to mistake symptom for cause. Populists sharpen and aim distrust, but they do not generate it from nothing. Their success depends on institutional environments already strained by continuity without consent and authority without visible consequence.

V. Embedded Autonomy and the Erosion of Consent

The experience described in the previous sections has a structural counterpart. What appears as unaccountable continuity is not simply inertia or secrecy, but a specific organizational condition: institutions that are insulated enough to act independently, yet insufficiently responsive to those they govern. Political theorist Peter Evans described this balance as "embedded autonomy"—a condition in which state institutions are protected from narrow interests while remaining connected to the social forces they are meant to serve.[2]

In its ideal form, embedded autonomy supports effective governance. Insulation allows institutions to resist short-term political pressure, preserve expertise, and pursue long-range objectives. Embeddedness ensures that this insulation does not harden into detachment. Institutions remain legible, responsive, and subject to feedback, even as they maintain operational independence.

Over time, this balance can drift. Autonomy persists, but embeddedness weakens. Institutions retain their insulation while their points of contact with public consent erode. Decision-making becomes increasingly internal, guided by professional norms, security rationales, or technocratic logics that are rarely explained in public-facing terms. Feedback is filtered, delayed, or absorbed without visible response.

From within the system, this drift is often understood as necessary. Complex environments demand continuity. Volatile politics requires stability. Expertise must be protected from interference. None of this implies conspiracy or coordinated intent. The system persists by operating according to its own internal logic.

From outside the system, the experience is different. Authority appears durable but distant, with decisions made by actors who are difficult to identify, challenge, or replace. Oversight exists, but it feels abstract. Consent is presumed rather than renewed. The state continues to function, but it no longer feels meaningfully connected to those it governs.

This is not a cabal, but a system that can function without active public understanding.

When autonomy becomes detached in this way, stability is no longer experienced as protection. It is experienced as exclusion. Institutions may remain lawful, professional, and procedurally sound, yet still feel anti-democratic in practice—not because they intend to subvert consent, but because they no longer rely on it as a condition of operation.

This structural condition helps explain why perceptions of a "deep state" persist even in the absence of secrecy or coordination. What citizens encounter is not hidden rule, but authority that appears insulated from pressure and unresponsive to participation. Embedded autonomy, once a source of strength, becomes indistinguishable from unaccountable power when its connection to public consent weakens.

VI. When the System No Longer Feels Yours

For many people, the sense that the system no longer belongs to them does not arrive as a conclusion. It arrives as an accumulation of repeated signals. Decisions are made and consequences follow, yet responsibility remains unclear. Errors are acknowledged indirectly, if at all, and apologies are rare.

One of the most powerful signals is the absence of reversal. When outcomes remain unchanged despite elections, protests, or public outcry, participation begins to feel symbolic. Engagement produces noise, not movement. Over time, this teaches a quiet lesson: input is registered, but it does not matter.

Another signal is the absence of ownership. When failures occur, responsibility disperses. Officials cite procedure, jurisdiction, or inherited constraints. Decisions are framed as unavoidable, the product of systems rather than choices. The result is not outrage so much as resignation. Power feels present everywhere and accountable nowhere.

This experience is reinforced by institutional distance. Authority speaks through documents, spokespeople, and formal statements, but rarely in a way that feels responsive or personal. Communication arrives polished and abstracted, stripped of acknowledgment or uncertainty. The tone suggests management rather than engagement. Citizens are addressed as audiences, not participants.

A kind of fog sets in. Reasons feel partial or overly technical, and key details remain unclear, classified, or deferred. Even when information is available, it does not cohere into understanding. The system appears legible in fragments but opaque as a whole.

What emerges from these conditions is not necessarily anger. It is estrangement. People begin to feel governed rather than represented. It begins to feel like something one lives under rather than within.

This is the experiential ground on which "deep state" belief takes hold. Not because people imagine secret rulers, but because the system feels unresponsive and beyond reach. The perception is less about hidden power than about inaccessible power—authority that persists without feedback and endures without renewal.

When institutions no longer feel like they belong to the public, legitimacy erodes quietly. The loss is not dramatic. It is gradual, cumulative, and difficult to articulate. What remains is a sense of distance that resists reassurance and deepens over time, shaping how all subsequent explanations are received.

VII. The Vocabulary Gap

One reason "deep state" belief persists is not the power of the myth itself, but the absence of a credible alternative. There is no widely shared public language for describing durable power that operates without secrecy or obvious illegality. When such power is experienced but not named, myth fills the gap.

The language institutions use to describe themselves is poorly suited to this task. Bureaucratic explanations rely on process, jurisdiction, and technical necessity. They speak in abstractions—mandates, frameworks, protocols—that may be accurate but feel emotionally vacant. These explanations describe *how* decisions were made, but rarely address what those decisions mean for people who experience them as imposed, repeated, or unchangeable.

As a result, official language often fails at the moment it is most needed. When authority feels distant, citizens are not only seeking information; they are seeking recognition. They want their experience of constraint, exclusion, or permanence to be acknowledged as real. Technical explanation, however precise, rarely performs that function. It clarifies procedure while leaving perception untouched.

Myth succeeds where bureaucracy fails because it is legible. It compresses complexity into intention. It offers a narrative in which power has agency, motive, and coherence. The story may be wrong in its particulars, but it feels complete in a way institutional language cannot. Where official explanations fragment responsibility, myth consolidates it.

This dynamic is reinforced by dismissal. When "deep state" belief is treated only as ignorance or paranoia, the underlying experience that produced it goes unanswered. Ridicule replaces explanation. The result is not correction, but entrenchment. Without a substitute vocabulary—one that can name persistence, insulation, and unresponsiveness without resorting to fantasy—the myth remains the most available explanation.

Dismissal without replacement reinforces belief It confirms the sense that official language is incapable of describing what people feel is happening to them. In that vacuum, myth does not merely survive; it becomes more credible than the abstractions offered in its place.

Until there is a public way to talk about power that persists without consent—plainly and without euphemism—bureaucratic explanation will continue to lose ground to stories that feel truer, even when they are not.

VIII. Implications

Belief in a "deep state" is not best understood as a claim about hidden rulers. It is a signal. It names the experience of living under institutions that feel insulated and unresponsive to participation. The language is imprecise, often exaggerated, and frequently wrong in detail—but the perception it expresses is rooted in lived encounter with durable authority.

Mockery misses the point. When the imagery is ridiculed, the experience that produced it is ignored. Dismissal treats belief as the problem rather than asking what conditions made that belief feel necessary. In doing so, it leaves the underlying sense of exclusion intact and reinforces the very suspicion it seeks to correct.

As long as power persists without visible explanation or renewal, myths of hidden control will remain credible. They will continue to outcompete bureaucratic language that cannot acknowledge permanence without euphemism or explain continuity without abstraction. The issue is not whether the myth is true, but why it feels truer than the official story.

Conclusion

This chapter has offered no solution because diagnosis must come first. Before mistrust can be understood across systems and cultures, the experience that gives rise to it must be taken seriously on its own terms. What follows shifts from this intuition to the deeper moral structures that shape how institutional failure is interpreted—why opacity is experienced as deception, and why continuity without consent so readily feels like betrayal.

REFERENCES

---

[1] Michael J. Glennon, *National Security and Double Government* (Oxford University Press, 2014).

[2] Peter Evans, *Embedded Autonomy: States and Industrial Transformation* (Princeton University Press, 1995).

Institutional failure is so often experienced as betrayal rather than malfunction. A malfunction implies a system that remains intelligible even when it breaks. Betrayal implies a violated expectation.

INTERLUDE

Moral Grammars and the Preconditions of Trust

This interlude's purpose is to name a missing analytic layer that helps explain why institutional failure in liberal democracies is so often experienced as betrayal rather than error. It does not offer a complete theory of moral authority or propose solutions. Rather, it clarifies a background assumption that is usually taken for granted—until it breaks.

I. From Opacity to Misrecognition: Why Institutional Failure Feels Like Deception

Institutional failure is often framed as an informational problem—delayed disclosure, partial transparency, or unclear explanation. But opacity alone does not explain why failure is so often experienced as deception, even when no explicit lie can be identified.

Many encounters between citizens and institutions are marked not simply by a lack of clarity, but by moral illegibility. People struggle to understand not only what decisions were made, but how those decisions relate to basic expectations about responsibility, restraint, and answerability. The result is misrecognition: institutions behave in ways that are formally correct yet experientially alien—so that even "accurate" disclosure can feel like withholding.

This dynamic builds directly on the conditions described in Chapter 5.5. When authority persists without visible renewal, when decisions endure across elections without explanation, and when accountability appears diffuse or symbolic, citizens are left to interpret behavior without a shared frame. The issue is not that institutions are always lying. It is that their actions no longer align with the expectations through which legitimacy is recognized.

Misrecognition arises when institutions and citizens operate according to different, unspoken assumptions about what authority owes those it governs. From the institutional perspective, continuity, procedure, and expertise may signal responsibility. From the citizen's perspective, the same signals can register as evasion, insulation, or indifference.

This helps explain why institutional failure is so often experienced as betrayal rather than malfunction. A malfunction implies a system that remains intelligible even when it breaks. Betrayal implies a violated expectation—an assumption about conduct that was never formally stated, but nonetheless relied upon. When institutions respond to failure with process alone, they may satisfy procedural requirements while deepening the sense that an implicit obligation has been ignored.

To understand why this dynamic produces mistrust that feels moral rather than technical, we need to name the background assumptions that structure how authority is interpreted in the first place. We need to identify the moral grammar at work.

II. What Is a Moral Grammar?

In philosophy, sociology, and anthropology, *moral grammar* often refers to implicit rules governing moral judgment or interaction. Here, I use the term differently. A moral grammar is not a set of values, beliefs, or doctrines, nor is it culture, ideology, or faith. It refers instead to the implicit assumptions that govern how authority is expected to behave and how legitimacy is recognized in practice. Like linguistic grammar, it operates largely beneath conscious awareness, shaping interpretation even when it is never explicitly taught.

Moral grammars organize expectations—within a given political and social context—about how authority should present and limit itself: about restraint, explanation, and answerability. They determine which actions feel legitimate, which failures feel tolerable, and which justifications feel sufficient. When these expectations are met, authority remains intelligible even when outcomes are contested; when they are not, its actions feel wrong in ways that are difficult to articulate.

These grammars are structural rather than expressive. They do not tell people *what* to believe, but they shape how people interpret behavior. They are revealed most clearly when they are broken. Just as grammatical errors disrupt comprehension even when the words are familiar, violations of moral grammar disrupt legitimacy even when procedures are followed.

Several expectations commonly embedded in liberal democratic governance illustrate this dynamic. There is an assumption that officials will tell the truth even when doing so is inconvenient. There is an expectation that power will restrain itself rather than push every advantage it is legally permitted to take. There is an assumption that explanation is owed, not optional. Authority is expected to remain answerable even when it is formally insulated.

These expectations are rarely codified or guaranteed by procedure. Instead, they function as background conditions— assumptions about how power *ought* to be exercised if it is to remain legitimate. Institutions rely on these assumptions without naming them, designing systems that presuppose their existence rather than reproducing them.

This is why moral grammar differs from morality in the conventional sense. It does not specify ethical ideals or prescribe virtuous behavior. It establishes the conditions under which authority can be recognized as legitimate without constant coercion or justification.

It also differs from norms, which prescribe appropriate behavior. Moral grammar operates at a deeper level: it structures how behavior is interpreted and recognized as legitimate in the first place, and it varies across political and social contexts rather than traveling easily between them.

When these conditions are met, governance feels intelligible even amid disagreement. When they are not, procedural correctness offers little reassurance.

The distinction can be clarified through a linguistic analogy:

Concept	Linguistic Equivalent	Role	Key Feature
Moral grammar	Deep grammar (syntax/structure)	Structures what counts as intelligible or legitimate	Largely implicit, context-dependent
Norms	Usage conventions (pragmatics)	Guide appropriate behavior in context	Semi-explicit, socially enforced
Morality	Semantics (meaning/content)	Defines values, principles, and judgments	Explicit, contestable

This analogy highlights the level at which moral grammar operates: not at the level of belief or rule, but at the level of interpretation.

Understanding moral grammar in this way helps clarify why institutional failure is often experienced as betrayal rather than error. What is perceived as broken is not only a rule or a process, but an unspoken expectation about how authority relates to those it governs. When that expectation is violated repeatedly, legitimacy erodes even if formal compliance remains intact.

III. Liberal Democracy's Hidden Assumption

Liberal democracy rests on an assumption it rarely states and no longer reliably sustains: that those who wield power will restrain themselves.[1] Its institutions are designed around procedures, rights, and checks, but they presuppose an internalized disposition toward limitation that precedes enforcement. Law is meant to catch violations, not to substitute for conscience.

This assumption is built into the architecture of liberal governance. Authority is fragmented rather than centralized. Discretion is delegated rather than eliminated. Oversight exists, but it is often indirect, delayed, or partial. These features make sense only if powerholders are expected to exercise judgment before they are compelled to do so. The system relies on restraint as a first line of defense.

In this design, internalized restraint functions as infrastructure. Not as private belief or ideology, but as a background expectation that actors will recognize obligations that exceed what is legally required. Officials are presumed to explain their actions even when not forced. They are expected to acknowledge error without coercion. They are assumed to limit the use of power not merely because they must, but because they should.

This design reflects a sequencing that is easy to overlook. Ethics precede procedure. Self-limitation precedes sanction. Liberal institutions do not attempt to monitor every action or anticipate every abuse. They assume that most powerholders will internalize limits and that formal mechanisms will address exceptions rather than serve as the primary constraint.

Liberal democracy remains stable only if most powerholders restrain themselves before the law is forced to restrain them.

When this assumption holds, governance can remain flexible, plural, and non-coercive. Institutions can tolerate disagreement and uncertainty because authority does not need to be constantly

---

[1] Here, "liberal democracy" refers to political systems that ground legitimacy in individual rights, procedural equality, and voluntary self-restraint rather than inherited authority or collective identity. These systems often speak in a language of neutrality—treating governance as technical and value-free—even as they depend on moral assumptions about conscience, restraint, and responsibility that neutrality itself cannot generate.

asserted or defended. Legitimacy accumulates through conduct rather than enforcement.

When the assumption weakens, however, the design becomes fragile. Procedures remain, but their moral grounding thins. Oversight expands to compensate for lost restraint. Compliance replaces judgment. What was meant to be a system of limited authority begins to feel like one of managed behavior.

This vulnerability is not a flaw introduced into liberal democracy. It is the cost of a system that privileges freedom over control and discretion over surveillance. The problem arises not when the assumption is acknowledged, but when it erodes without being named. Institutions continue to operate as if restraint were intact, even as behavior signals otherwise.

Understanding this hidden assumption helps explain why institutional failure is experienced not simply as inefficiency or error, but as a deeper rupture. What appears broken is not only a rule or a policy, but the expectation that authority would limit itself before being forced to do so. When that expectation collapses, trust no longer operates through familiar expectations.

IV. What Happens When the Moral Grammar Erodes

When the moral grammar that underwrites liberal democratic authority weakens, institutions do not simply stop functioning. They adapt. But what they substitute for lost restraint is not equivalent to what has eroded, and its effects are often experienced as distortion rather than repair.

As internal restraint thins, institutions compensate with procedure. Rules multiply. Compliance mechanisms expand. Oversight becomes more formalized, more documented, and more insulated. Authority increasingly justifies itself through process rather than judgment. Decisions are defended as correct because they followed protocol, not because they can be explained in terms that resonate with shared expectations.

Accountability shifts accordingly. Where responsibility was once understood as ethical—an obligation to acknowledge error, justify action, and accept consequence—it becomes administrative. Compliance replaces ownership. Errors are reframed as procedural misalignments rather than failures of judgment. Correction occurs internally, if at all, and rarely in ways that are legible to those affected.

Transparency undergoes a similar transformation. Instead of explanation, institutions offer disclosure. Information is released without narrative continuity, context, or acknowledgment. The burden of interpretation shifts to the public, even as the conditions for interpretation deteriorate. What is technically visible remains experientially opaque.

This shift from moral authority to administrative control does not require deception. It follows naturally from systems attempting to govern without relying on internalized restraint. But from the outside, the effect can feel indistinguishable from evasion. Institutions appear to speak without answering, to disclose without explaining, and to correct without admitting fault.

It is in environments like this that conspiratorial narratives can gain traction. They do not arise from ignorance or irrationality alone. They arise because they restore elements that administrative language has stripped away. Conspiracies reintroduce motive where procedure appears impersonal. They supply agency where responsibility has been diffused. They impose coherence where explanation has fragmented.

This does not make conspiracism accurate or justify its conclusions. When institutions cease to offer morally intelligible accounts of their actions, people reach for narratives that do—even if those narratives exaggerate intent, personalize structure, or misidentify cause.

The danger is not that conspiracies compete with facts, but that they compete with the absence of morally intelligible explanation. When such explanation weakens, intentional narratives move in to supply coherence. The result is not merely misinformation, but a deeper displacement: power is interpreted through suspicion because it no longer speaks in a register that can be recognized as accountable.

This erosion does not announce itself as collapse. It appears as drift. Procedures continue. Authority persists. Yet the grammar through which legitimacy is recognized no longer holds. What remains is a system that functions, but no longer explains itself in ways that align with inherited expectations of authority. In that gap, trust does not simply decline; it reorganizes around suspicion.

V. Why This Failure Is Not Universal

The erosion described here is most acute in political systems that rely heavily on internalized restraint rather than overt enforcement.

Different political orders embed authority within distinct moral architectures. Some systems emphasize collective identity or peoplehood as the primary source of legitimacy. Others rely more openly on hierarchy, coercion, or centralized control. In such contexts, expectations about explanation, restraint, and answerability differ. Authority may be experienced as harsh or unjust, but it is not necessarily experienced as illegible.

Liberal democracies are distinctive in this respect. They presume a high degree of moral self-regulation among powerholders while minimizing overt enforcement. They rely on explanation rather than command, justification rather than decree. When these assumptions hold, authority can remain limited without becoming fragile. When they erode, however, the effects are felt not only as political failure but as epistemic breakdown.

This is why similar levels of institutional opacity can produce different responses across societies. Where moral grammar aligns with administrative practice, opacity may be tolerated as necessity. Where that grammar weakens, the same opacity is experienced as deception. What changes is not simply the amount of information available, but the interpretive framework through which authority is judged.

When the moral grammar that underwrites liberal democratic authority weakens, institutional failure is experienced as epistemic breakdown. Decisions may remain lawful and procedures intact, yet the connection between authority and understanding weakens.

None of this implies that other systems are healthier or more just; it means only that the relationship between authority and understanding is structured differently. Mistrust, in these cases, reflects a specific mismatch between inherited expectations and contemporary institutional behavior, rather than a universal pathology of modern governance.

VI. Reading Mistrust as a Signal

Much of contemporary mistrust is communicated poorly. People struggle to describe what feels wrong, and the language they use often obscures more than it clarifies. Claims are exaggerated, motives are personalized, and structural conditions are reduced to intentional plots. From the standpoint of accuracy, these explanations are frequently mistaken.

Yet the intuition behind them is often coherent.

When citizens say "they're lying," "it's all rigged," they are not usually offering a falsifiable account of events. They are expressing a perception that authority no longer behaves in ways that feel recognizable or answerable. What is being signaled is not secret knowledge, but a breakdown in moral legibility.

This distinction matters. Treating mistrust solely as delusion or misinformation misses the information it contains. Mistrust functions as a diagnostic response to repeated experiences of opacity, continuity without consent, and accountability that feels symbolic rather than real. People may misidentify causes, but they are often responding accurately to effects.

At the same time, recognizing mistrust as a signal does not require accepting its explanations. Intuition is not evidence. Feeling wronged does not make a narrative correct. Many accounts of institutional behavior substitute intention for structure, coherence for complexity, and agency for process. These substitutions distort reality even as they attempt to restore meaning.

The analytic task is to separate the signal—the experience of misalignment—from the story built to explain it. The signal reflects a gap between institutional behavior and inherited expectations of authority; the story attempts to resolve that gap using the narrative tools available. When those tools are crude or conspiratorial, the explanation fails even if the underlying intuition remains grounded.

Reading mistrust as a signal allows for this separation. It acknowledges that something has broken without endorsing the accounts built to explain the break. It treats suspicion as a response to experience rather than as proof of hidden coordination. In doing so, it preserves the possibility of diagnosis without collapsing into either dismissal or validation.

This framing is essential for what follows. If mistrust is treated only as pathology, the cases that follow appear irrational or culturally idiosyncratic. If it is treated as truth, they collapse into accusation. Reading mistrust as a signal instead opens a different path. It allows us to examine how similar intuitions emerge across different moral grammars and political systems—without dismissing them as error or accepting them as fact.

VII. Transition

The dynamics described in this interlude are not unique to any single country. They are structural rather than cultural, rooted in how authority is morally organized and how legitimacy is expected to operate. What varies across societies is not whether mistrust emerges, but how it is interpreted, expressed, and mobilized.

Different political systems rely on different moral grammars. Some emphasize collective identity, others hierarchy or coercion, others procedural legality. These differences shape how institutional failure is experienced and what kinds of narratives arise in response. Where moral authority is grounded in restraint and explanation, erosion produces epistemic confusion. Where it is grounded elsewhere, mistrust takes different forms.

The chapters that follow examine these variations directly. By looking beyond a single national context, they show how similar pressures—opacity, continuity, and unaccountable power— generate distinct patterns of mistrust under different moral architectures. The goal is not to rank systems or diagnose cultural pathology, but to understand how institutional design and moral expectation interact.

To understand mistrust globally, we must examine how societies organize moral authority—and what happens when it breaks down.

The forms differ; the fractures are familiar.

CHAPTER 7

Global Case Studies

Mistrust in the United States, Brazil, India, and
Russia, with an aside on Europe

Distrust of institutions and the proliferation of conspiracy belief are often treated as uniquely American pathologies—products of polarization, media fragmentation, or declining civic norms in the United States. This framing is both empirically inaccurate and analytically limiting.[1] What varies is not the presence of distrust, but how it is expressed, justified, and mobilized.

This chapter examines how conspiracy belief and institutional mistrust manifest across four distinct national contexts: the United States, Brazil, India, and Russia. It also includes a brief comparative aside on Europe as an intermediate case, illustrating how institutional "buffering" can moderate—without eliminating—epistemic collapse. These cases were selected not to suggest equivalence, but to illustrate variation within a shared structural condition. Each country differs in regime type, media environment, historical memory, and cultural logic. Yet in each case, conspiratorial narratives gain traction where institutions appear opaque, exclusionary, or unaccountable—and where official explanations fail to align with lived experience.[2]

The purpose of this chapter is threefold. First, it demonstrates that modern mistrust is not an American anomaly, but a global symptom of governance drift, digital disruption, and declining institutional legitimacy. Second, it shows how conspiracy narratives adapt to local histories and cultural frames while responding to similar structural pressures—epistemic opacity, elite impunity, and unresolved betrayal. Third, it illuminates how conspiratorial belief often emerges not from ignorance alone, but from real exclusions: populations who experience power without representation, authority without accountability, and explanation without recognition.

Comparative analysis reveals an important distinction. While the *content* of conspiracy narratives varies—drawing on national myths, historical grievances, or ideological conflicts—the *conditions* that sustain them recur. Transitional democracies exhibit conspiracism shaped by unresolved authoritarian legacies. Hybrid regimes weaponize conspiratorial logic as a tool of governance. Established democracies experience fragmentation as institutional credibility erodes under informational overload and political polarization. The forms differ; the fractures are familiar.

By situating conspiracism within these broader patterns, this chapter reframes belief as a relational phenomenon rather than a cultural defect. Conspiracy narratives do not arise in a vacuum; they take shape where institutions lose the capacity to speak credibly and citizens must interpret power without reliable frameworks. In such environments, suspicion becomes a shared language—one that can mobilize, mislead, or both.

This chapter does not validate conspiratorial claims or excuse their harms. It examines why such narratives persist across contexts, how they vary across societies, and what that variation reveals about the structural conditions under which mistrust takes hold.

I. Why Global Case Studies Matter

Distrust is often explained as a product of national culture, partisan polarization, or local media dysfunction. Comparative analysis reveals a more durable insight: distrust is structural, not merely cultural, and it adapts to local histories rather than emerging from them wholesale.

Global case studies make it possible to distinguish between surface variation and underlying cause. Political traditions, religious narratives, and historical memory shape the content of conspiracy belief, but the conditions that sustain it recur with striking consistency. Across political systems, conspiratorial narratives gain traction where institutions are experienced as opaque, exclusionary, or unaccountable—particularly when past betrayals remain unresolved or responsibility is diffused without consequence.

Comparison also clarifies the limits of purely psychological or informational explanations. If conspiracism were driven mainly by cognitive bias or misinformation, its intensity would vary unpredictably across contexts. Instead, it clusters around familiar fractures: exclusion, elite impunity, contradictory official narratives, and communication environments that reward suspicion over explanation.

At the same time, comparison reveals how cultural logics shape interpretation. In some societies, conspiracism is filtered through nationalist mythologies or civilizational narratives; in others, through histories of colonialism, surveillance, or systemic neglect. These frames do not generate conspiracism on their own. They function as interpretive lenses, translating shared structural conditions into locally intelligible narratives of betrayal or control.

Without comparison, conspiratorial belief is easily misdiagnosed as cultural pathology. With it, mistrust becomes legible as a patterned response to institutional environments that fail to generate credibility. What differs is not its presence, but the language through which it is expressed and the political uses to which it is put.

Global case studies therefore sharpen rather than relativize the problem. They show that mistrust is predictable under certain conditions—conditions that recur across contexts even as their expression varies.

II. United States: Betrayal and Belief

In the United States, conspiracism emerges from a volatile convergence of historical betrayal, institutional fragmentation, and informational saturation. The American case is defined by decentralization: distrust proliferates across multiple institutions simultaneously, without a single authoritative narrative capable of containing it. Scholars have long noted the persistence of conspiracy belief in American political life. The contemporary landscape, however, reflects a different configuration. It is shaped less by enduring suspicion alone than by the erosion of shared standards for evaluating authority.

The contemporary American conspiratorial landscape is expansive: QAnon, election fraud narratives, vaccine skepticism, intelligence secrecy surrounding the Kennedy assassination, and enduring suspicion of federal agencies all coexist within a fragmented epistemic ecosystem. These beliefs vary widely in content, yet they share a common orientation: the conviction that official explanations systematically obscure deeper truths. This conviction does not arise in a historical vacuum.

The United States possesses a long and well-documented record of real institutional conspiracies. These include coordinated deception, withheld knowledge, and delayed accountability, all of which have recalibrated public expectations of authority. As examined in Chapter 3, episodes such as COINTELPRO, the Tuskegee syphilis study, MKUltra, documented CIA relationships with media organizations, and corporate suppression of known harms were not speculative fantasies. They were documented cases of institutional wrongdoing revealed only after prolonged denial. The epistemic residue of these betrayals continues to shape public expectations of authority.[3] For many Americans, disbelief is not a reflex but a lesson learned.

This legacy intersects with uniquely American structural features. A privatized healthcare system, sprawling and opaque bureaucracies, aggressive corporate lobbying, and extreme media fragmentation place extraordinary epistemic burdens on citizens. Individuals are routinely asked to make high-stakes decisions—about health, risk, legality, and political legitimacy—without transparent access to the information shaping those decisions. Trust becomes conditional, situational, and increasingly brittle.[4]

Marginalized communities experience this alienation with particular intensity. For Black Americans, the memory of medical exploitation and discriminatory governance renders official reassurances about safety or intent morally insufficient. For military veterans, revelations surrounding Agent Orange exposure (a toxic defoliant used during the Vietnam War), alongside burn pit exposure in Iraq and Afghanistan and the delayed recognition of harm, reinforce the belief that institutional care often follows, rather than prevents, damage. In rural communities devastated by the opioid crisis, corporate and regulatory failures have made skepticism toward pharmaceutical authority a rational posture rather than a fringe belief.[5]

What distinguishes the United States is not simply the presence of conspiratorial belief, but its pluralization. No single narrative dominates. Instead, conspiracism functions as a distributed epistemic style—an orientation toward authority characterized by preemptive doubt. Digital platforms accelerate this process by allowing disparate suspicions to coexist, cross-pollinate, and reinforce one another without requiring coherence. Contradiction does not weaken belief; it broadens it.

Political entrepreneurs exploit this environment by selectively validating distrust without resolving it. Claims of election fraud, for example, need not be proven to be effective. Their function is anticipatory: to frame loss as theft and accountability as persecution. Once institutional credibility is sufficiently weakened, evidence becomes secondary to allegiance. The result is not universal disbelief, but epistemic factionalism—competing realities grounded in divergent trust networks.

The American case thus illustrates a distinctive danger. When distrust is both historically grounded and structurally amplified, conspiracism does not merely oppose authority; it fragments it. American conspiracism destabilizes institutions without replacing them. Authority erodes horizontally, leaving governance contested and legitimacy increasingly conditional, with truth often filtered through identity-based trust networks rather than shared procedural standards.[6]

The lesson is not that Americans are uniquely prone to irrational belief. It is that a society with a documented history of institutional betrayal, combined with radical informational decentralization and a highly permissive speech environment, creates conditions in which belief detaches from shared standards of validation. In such an environment, conspiracism becomes less a deviation from democratic norms than a symptom of their erosion.

III. Brazil: The Populist Paradox

Brazil illustrates a central paradox of contemporary conspiracism: narratives that emerge from legitimate distrust can be mobilized both to challenge elite impunity and to erode democratic accountability. Under President Jair Bolsonaro, conspiracy rhetoric did not arise on the political margins alone; it was actively weaponized from within the executive, transforming suspicion into a governing style.

Bolsonaro's discourse repeatedly framed Brazil's institutions as compromised by hidden enemies. Courts, electoral authorities, journalists, public health officials, and international organizations were portrayed as components of a corrupt "system" working against the nation's authentic will. During the COVID-19 pandemic, this rhetoric intensified. Scientific guidance was cast as globalist manipulation, public health measures as authoritarian control, and vaccine campaigns as plots against national sovereignty. These claims were not merely fringe speculation; they were amplified by state authority and normalized through repetition.[7]

This strategy resonated in part because it tapped into preexisting institutional distrust. Brazil's democratic institutions, though formally consolidated after the end of military rule in 1985, have struggled to overcome the legacy of authoritarianism, corruption, and elite impunity. The military dictatorship left behind unresolved abuses, limited accountability, and a persistent perception that powerful actors operate above the law. Subsequent corruption scandals—most notably those revealed by Operation Car Wash, a sweeping investigation (launched in 2014) into bribery and kickbacks involving political and corporate elites—reinforced the belief that political and economic elites collude while ordinary citizens bear the cost.[8]

These memories do not mechanically produce conspiracism, but they provide a symbolic reservoir from which it draws. Contemporary conflicts are layered onto older narratives of betrayal and resistance, giving present-day suspicion a civilizational depth that extends beyond partisan politics.

Bolsonaro's repeated attacks on Brazil's electoral system exemplify this pattern. Without providing evidence of systemic fraud, he cast doubt on voting machines and warned of stolen elections well before ballots were cast. These claims did not require proof to be effective. They functioned as anticipatory delegitimation, preparing supporters to interpret any unfavorable outcome as confirmation of conspiracy rather than democratic loss.[9] Distrust became preemptive.

Digital platforms played a critical amplifying role. WhatsApp, Facebook, and Telegram facilitated rapid circulation of conspiratorial narratives, often within closed networks resistant to correction. The content itself varied—from pandemic misinformation to electoral paranoia—but the underlying logic remained consistent: institutions lie; only the leader tells the truth. Algorithmic and peer-to-peer amplification allowed suspicion to circulate faster than verification, reinforcing affective loyalty over procedural legitimacy.[10]

Brazil's case demonstrates that conspiracism is not inherently anti-institutional. It can be selectively deployed to weaken specific institutions while strengthening executive authority. The paradox lies in its appeal: conspiratorial narratives flourish by invoking democratic distrust, yet their political effect is often to hollow out democratic safeguards. What begins as skepticism toward elite impunity can end as acceptance of unchecked power.

This pattern underscores a central theme of this book. Conspiracism does not simply oppose authority; it reconfigures it. In Brazil, distrust did not dissolve political order—it was reorganized around a populist figure who claimed to embody transparency while undermining the institutions designed to ensure it. The lesson is not that Brazilian society is uniquely vulnerable to conspiratorial belief, but that unresolved institutional legitimacy creates conditions in which suspicion can be transformed into a tool of governance.

IV. India: Distrust as Nationalism

In India, conspiracism operates less as a challenge to power than as a mechanism for national consolidation. Under Prime Minister Narendra Modi and the Bharatiya Janata Party (BJP), conspiracy narratives have been woven into a broader ideological project that frames dissent, institutional failure, and social unrest as the product of hidden enemies acting against the nation. Suspicion is not merely tolerated; it is politically reinforced in ways that can serve legitimation.

Government-aligned rhetoric frequently invokes plots by "anti-national" forces, foreign actors, secular elites, or internal saboteurs accused of undermining India's unity and Hindu civilizational identity. Policy failures, economic disruption, and administrative breakdowns are recast not as governance shortcomings but as the effects of deliberate obstruction. In this framework, criticism becomes evidence of conspiracy, and accountability is displaced by accusation.[11]

This dynamic has particular force because it resonates with deep historical memory. India's colonial experience produced enduring narratives of foreign manipulation, cultural erosion, and elite collaboration with outside power. These memories do not mechanically generate conspiracism, but they provide a symbolic reservoir from which contemporary narratives draw. Modern political struggles are overlaid onto older stories of betrayal and resistance, giving contemporary suspicion a civilizational depth that transcends partisan politics.[12]

Conspiratorial framing in India thus performs a distinctive function: it redefines loyalty. To question the state is not merely to oppose a government, but to stand outside the nation itself. Dissenting journalists, academics, activists, and minority communities are portrayed as vectors of destabilization rather than participants in democratic deliberation. This reframing transforms skepticism downward—toward citizens—while insulating authority upward.

Digital communication systems have amplified these dynamics dramatically. Encrypted messaging platforms such as WhatsApp have become central conduits for rumor and conspiratorial claims. False reports of kidnappings, religious desecration, or foreign plots have circulated rapidly within closed networks, sometimes contributing to real-world violence and vigilantism. In these cases, conspiratorial belief does not remain discursive; it becomes operational.[13]

What distinguishes the Indian case is not simply the prevalence of misinformation, but its integration into nationalist narrative structure. Conspiracy is not an alternative explanation competing with official accounts; it is often aligned with them. State silence, selective enforcement, or rhetorical endorsement allows suspicion to flourish without formal validation. The boundary between popular rumor and political messaging becomes functionally porous.

This alignment alters the moral logic of conspiracism. Rather than positioning believers as outsiders resisting a corrupt system, conspiratorial narratives in India frequently position believers as defenders of order against hidden chaos. Suspicion is framed as vigilance, exclusion as protection, and repression as necessity. In this way, conspiracism becomes a language through which power explains itself, rather than a language through which it is challenged.

India's case underscores a crucial comparative insight. Conspiratorial belief does not always emerge from institutional weakness alone. It can also arise from institutional strength deployed without epistemic restraint—where authority is confident, communicatively dominant, and shielded from accountability. Under such conditions, distrust is not directed upward toward power, but outward toward designated internal enemies. The result is not democratic erosion through collapse, but through consolidation—an epistemic narrowing that renders pluralism suspect and dissent dangerous.[14]

V. Russia: The Performance of Paranoia

In Russia, conspiracism functions neither primarily as popular resistance nor as nationalist consolidation, but as a governing performance. Under Vladimir Putin, suspicion is not merely tolerated or instrumentalized—it is cultivated as an ambient condition of political life. The Russian state is less focused on persuading citizens of a single coherent narrative than on sustaining epistemic instability itself.

State-sponsored disinformation and managed media ecosystems generate a constant churn of contradictory explanations. Official narratives shift, overlap, and cancel one another without apology. Western governments are portrayed simultaneously as incompetent and omnipotent, decadent and threatening, weak yet conspiratorial. The effect is not belief in a particular claim, but resignation to the idea that truth itself is strategic.[15]

This approach reflects a post-Soviet epistemology shaped by decades of institutional deception. Under late Soviet rule, public discourse operated under conditions of near-universal disbelief. Citizens learned not to trust official narratives, but also not to expect alternatives that were more reliable. The collapse of the Soviet Union did not restore epistemic trust; it entrenched cynicism.[16] The prevailing logic became: *everyone lies—we merely choose which lies serve us best.*

Putin's regime has leveraged this inherited cynicism as a method of control. Rather than suppress all dissent, the state permits a managed plurality of narratives, including conspiracy theories, controlled opposition, and pseudo-critical voices.

Externally, Russian disinformation campaigns exploit this logic by amplifying mistrust abroad. The objective is not to convince foreign audiences of Russia's innocence, but to undermine confidence in their own institutions. Messages emphasize hypocrisy, historical wrongdoing, and elite manipulation: *your leaders lie too.* The strategy is epistemic sabotage—weakening belief in truth rather than advancing an alternative one.[17]

Internally, conspiratorial narratives serve a different purpose. They normalize suspicion as realism. Citizens are encouraged to view politics as an arena of hidden struggle among elites, intelligence services, and foreign powers—an arena in which ordinary people have little agency. In this worldview, transparency is naïve, reform is illusory, and loyalty is pragmatic rather than principled. Conspiracism becomes not a challenge to authority, but a justification for endurance.

Crucially, this system does not depend on citizens believing the state. It depends on citizens believing that belief itself is futile. When all narratives appear manipulative, withdrawal becomes rational. Political disengagement is reframed as wisdom. Cynicism masquerades as sophistication.

Russia thus illustrates a distinctive endpoint of epistemic opacity: not fragmentation, but saturation. Truth is not denied outright; it is drowned. Authority is preserved not through credibility, but through exhaustion. In such conditions, conspiracism ceases to function as a language of protest and becomes a shared cultural posture—one that insulates power by convincing citizens that no alternative epistemic order is possible.[18]

VI. A Note on Europe: Buffering Institutions Without Immunity

Europe is not treated here as a fifth full case study, but as a contrast case that helps clarify why conspiracism escalates more rapidly when everyday governance is experienced as opaque, punitive, or procedurally illegible. It is omitted from the core set not because it is immune, but because it occupies a structurally intermediate position in the global landscape of mistrust. Across much of Europe, conspiracy beliefs have proliferated in recent years—vaccine skepticism, anti-immigrant paranoia, "deep state" narratives aimed at the European Union, and populist suspicion of courts, experts, and journalists are all well documented—yet these dynamics have generally been less destabilizing than in the cases examined above.

This difference is not cultural or the result of superior civic virtue. Rather, it reflects the persistence—however strained—of institutional buffering mechanisms that moderate epistemic collapse. Many European states retain relatively trusted civil services, universal healthcare systems, strong public broadcasters, and administrative continuity that reduces opacity in everyday governance. These features do not eliminate distrust, but they constrain its escalation.

As a result, conspiracism in Europe tends to plateau rather than metastasize. It appears episodically rather than systemically, often clustering around specific crises—such as COVID-19 restrictions in Germany and France, or migration debates in Italy and Sweden—rather than reorganizing the entire epistemic order. Populist movements exploit suspicion, but they face countervailing institutions that remain partially credible and procedurally legible. Even where trust erodes, shared standards of authority have not fully collapsed.

This buffering effect is uneven and fragile. In parts of Eastern and Southern Europe, where institutional legitimacy is weaker and historical grievances sharper, conspiratorial narratives have exerted greater political force. Hungary and Poland illustrate how quickly this moderation can erode when judicial independence, media pluralism, and administrative neutrality are deliberately weakened. Europe, then, should not be read as a zone of immunity, but as a warning case: where epistemic governance holds, conspiracism is contained; where it deteriorates, familiar patterns reemerge.

Europe's role in this chapter is therefore illustrative rather than diagnostic. It shows that conspiracism scales with institutional opacity rather than national temperament. Where institutions remain visible, accountable, and procedurally consistent, distrust remains contested rather than total. Where those conditions weaken, conspiratorial logic rapidly fills the gap.

VII. Shared Patterns Across Borders

Despite wide variation in political systems, cultural traditions, and historical experience, the cases examined in this chapter reveal a convergence of underlying conditions. Conspiracism does not arise randomly or track national temperament alone. It clusters predictably around recurring structural failures, adapting to local contexts while preserving a common logic.

The first of these conditions is institutional betrayal, whether real, perceived, or unresolved. In Brazil and the United States, documented corruption and delayed accountability have left durable epistemic scars. In India and Russia, historical experience has normalized suspicion toward official narratives. In each case, past failures shape present interpretation. Trust, once broken without repair, does not reset; it accumulates as memory. Conspiratorial belief often functions as vigilance in environments where institutional reassurance has proven unreliable.

A second shared condition is exclusion from meaningful decision-making. Conspiratorial narratives flourish where large segments of the population experience power as distant, unresponsive, or insulated from consequence. Where participation feels symbolic and accountability abstract, suspicion becomes a rational interpretive stance.

Third, conspiracism intensifies under conditions of elite impunity and symbolic double standards. When elites appear exempt from the rules governing ordinary citizens, official explanations lose moral credibility—even when factually accurate. In such environments, people ask less whether institutions are correct than whether they are sincere.

A fourth recurring pattern is narrative incoherence from authority. Contradictory messaging, premature certainty followed by quiet revision, and selective transparency undermine credibility across regimes. Where explanations shift without acknowledgment, audiences learn to treat confidence as performative rather than informative. Conspiratorial narratives exploit this gap by offering coherence where official accounts appear unstable.

Finally, all cases operate within digital environments that reward doubt, outrage, and moral clarity more reliably than restraint or uncertainty. These systems do not create conspiracism, but they accelerate its spread and intensify its appeal. Fragmentation replaces shared exposure; repetition substitutes for verification.

Taken together, these conditions reveal conspiracism as a structural response to failures of epistemic governance. It emerges where institutions cannot sustain credibility—where authority is exercised without legibility, accountability, or reciprocal trust. The narratives differ, but the underlying conditions recur with striking consistency.

This carries a clear implication: conspiracism is not primarily a function of misinformation, cultural irrationality, or extremism. Its persistence across disparate contexts points instead to a breakdown in how institutions explain themselves and maintain credibility. Where explanation fails, belief migrates. Suspicion becomes portable, adaptable, and globally intelligible.

Without addressing these conditions, efforts to suppress conspiratorial belief will continue to misfire—treating symptoms while leaving the underlying environment unchanged.

VIII. Conspiracy as a Language of the Disenfranchised

Once structural mistrust takes hold, conspiratorial belief often functions less as a rejection of reality than as a way of making sense of it. Rather than arising only from false belief, conspiracy narratives provide a framework through which lived exclusion becomes intelligible. They are often embraced not because they are demonstrably true, but because they render power legible in environments where authority feels opaque and accountability elusive.

Disenfranchisement in this context is epistemic as much as political. It describes the experience of being affected by decisions whose reasoning feels inaccessible, dismissive, or morally incomplete. When institutional language becomes procedural and abstract, it ceases to function as a shared explanatory framework. Conspiracy narratives respond by personalizing structure—naming agents where institutions describe systems.

In this sense, conspiracism operates as a vernacular epistemology—a grassroots method of making power intelligible when official explanations feel incomplete or evasive. It translates systemic failure into intentional action, imposing design and purpose where institutions describe contingency. Where institutions explain outcomes as emergent, accidental, or probabilistic, conspiratorial narratives insist that someone must be responsible. This insistence is not primarily epistemic; it is moral. It reflects a demand for accountability in contexts where responsibility appears perpetually deferred.

The appeal of such narratives is especially strong in societies undergoing rapid transformation or institutional decay. Transitional democracies, hybrid regimes, and highly unequal societies often produce outcomes that feel arbitrary to those most affected by them. Economic dislocation, public health crises, security failures, and administrative neglect impose real costs without clear explanation. When official accounts emphasize systemic constraints rather than agency, conspiracy narratives restore a sense—however illusory—of causality.

This does not mean that conspiratorial belief is benign. The moral clarity it provides often comes at the expense of accuracy, pluralism, and social trust. It simplifies complex phenomena into antagonistic binaries and redirects anger toward scapegoated groups. Yet dismissing conspiracism as mere irrationality obscures why it resonates. It persists because it performs epistemic work that institutions increasingly fail to do: making power legible to those who experience its consequences most acutely.

Importantly, conspiracism as a language of the disenfranchised is not confined to any single ideology or political orientation. It appears on the right and the left, among majorities and minorities, within democracies and authoritarian states alike. What unites these expressions is not shared belief content, but shared conditions of epistemic exclusion—the experience of being affected by decisions that are explained poorly, justified weakly, or insulated from challenge.

Understanding conspiracism in this way reframes the normative problem. The central issue is not simply that false beliefs circulate, but that large numbers of people lack access to authoritative narratives that acknowledge their experiences while remaining accountable to evidence. Until institutions can once again speak credibly to those they govern—not only by asserting expertise, but by making power legible—conspiratorial narratives will continue to function as alternative vocabularies of meaning.

This insight carries a warning. Efforts to suppress conspiratorial belief without addressing the conditions that sustain it risk deepening mistrust rather than resolving it. When the available language for expressing grievance is delegitimized, grievance does not disappear; it radicalizes. The task is not to validate conspiratorial claims, but to rebuild institutional communication capable of explaining harm without evasion and authority without contempt.

Conclusion

The cases examined in this chapter show that conspiracism is best understood not as a cultural anomaly or informational failure, but as a structural response to environments in which authority becomes opaque, unaccountable, or difficult to interpret. Across divergent political systems, conspiracy narratives emerge where institutions lose the capacity to explain themselves in ways that remain credible to those they govern.

These cases also demonstrate that conspiracism is not politically uniform. It can be mobilized against institutions, embedded within them, or diffused across fragmented publics. What varies is not the presence of mistrust, but how it is organized—whether it destabilizes authority, consolidates it, or renders it incoherent.

The central challenge, then, is not simply the correction of false belief, but the restoration of epistemic credibility. Where institutions cannot make power legible, acknowledge uncertainty, and sustain accountability, distrust does not disappear—it adapts. Under such conditions, conspiratorial reasoning becomes less a deviation than a competing mode of interpretation.

This has implications beyond the specific cases examined here. In an environment shaped by informational fragmentation and declining institutional legitimacy, conspiracism functions as a transferable language of mistrust—one that can travel across contexts even as its content changes.

The next chapter turns to a related but necessary question: how institutional drift and accountability vacuums reshape these conditions—and amplify the very dynamics this chapter has sought to clarify.

REFERENCES

1 Pippa Norris, *Critical Citizens: Global Support for Democratic Governance* (Oxford University Press, 1999).

2 Francis Fukuyama, *Trust: The Social Virtues and the Creation of Prosperity* (Free Press, 1995).

3 Kathryn S. Olmsted, *Real Enemies: Conspiracy Theories and American Democracy, World War I to 9/11* (Oxford University Press, 2009).

4 Jacob S. Hacker and Paul Pierson, *Winner-Take-All Politics* (Simon & Schuster, 2010).

5 Harriet A. Washington, *Medical Apartheid* (Doubleday, 2006).

6 Steven Levitsky and Daniel Ziblatt, *How Democracies Die* (Crown, 2018).

7 Cas Mudde and Cristóbal Rovira Kaltwasser, *Populism: A Very Short Introduction* (Oxford University Press, 2017).

8 Alfred Stepan, *Rethinking Military Politics: Brazil and the Southern Cone* (Princeton University Press, 1988).

9 Steven Levitsky and Daniel Ziblatt, *How Democracies Die* (Crown, 2018).

10 David Nemer, *Technology of the Oppressed* (MIT Press, 2022).

11 Christophe Jaffrelot, *Modi's India: Hindu Nationalism and the Rise of Ethnic Democracy* (Princeton University Press, 2021).

12 Partha Chatterjee, *The Nation and Its Fragments* (Princeton University Press, 1993).

13 Amrita Basu, "Hindu Nationalism, Social Media, and the Mobilization of Violence," *Journal of Asian Studies* 78, no. 3 (2019).

14 Arjun Appadurai, *Fear of Small Numbers* (Duke University Press, 2006).

15 Peter Pomerantsev, *Nothing Is True and Everything Is Possible* (PublicAffairs, 2014).

16 Alexei Yurchak, *Everything Was Forever, Until It Was No More* (Princeton University Press, 2006).

17 Ben Nimmo, "Anatomy of an Information War," *NATO Strategic Communications Centre of Excellence* (2015).

18 Timur Kuran, *Private Truths, Public Lies* (Harvard University Press, 1995).

CHAPTER 8

The Conspiracy Spectrum

Differentiating Between Legitimate Skepticism and
Harmful Paranoia

Public discourse often treats conspiracy belief as a single phenomenon: irrational, dangerous, and opposed to reason. In this framing, claims are either true or false, believers either rational or deluded, and skepticism itself becomes suspect. This binary has intuitive appeal, but obscures more than it clarifies, collapsing fundamentally different forms of disbelief into a single category.

As the previous chapters have shown, distrust does not arise in a vacuum. It emerges under specific conditions, often as a response to opacity, exclusion, and unresolved betrayal. Yet acknowledging the structural origins of mistrust does not require treating all conspiratorial beliefs as equal. The analytic task is to distinguish between warranted skepticism and corrosive paranoia without defaulting to dismissal or repression.

This chapter argues that such distinctions require moving beyond a binary framework. Conspiratorial thinking is better understood as existing along a spectrum of legitimacy, ranging from empirically grounded claims about real, documented conspiracies to, at the other extreme, self-sealing or weaponized belief systems that are detached from evidence and resistant to correction. Between these poles lie narratives that vary in evidentiary support, openness to revision, and potential for harm. These forms differ not only in their factual basis, but in how they relate to reality, accountability, and the possibility of being proven wrong.

Adopting a spectrum accomplishes three tasks. First, it protects legitimate inquiry: documented conspiracies and reasonable suspicion—often vindicated only after prolonged denial—are part of historical reality, not deviations from it. Second, it clarifies epistemic and moral stakes, distinguishing evidence-based skepticism from belief that becomes self-sealing, scapegoating, or detached from correction. Third, it provides a framework for response.

Crucially, conspiratorial beliefs are not static. They move along this spectrum over time, shaped by new evidence, institutional behavior, political incentives, and social reinforcement. Claims once dismissed may later prove credible; others may harden into dogma when inquiry is suppressed or grievance is exploited.

In an age of epistemic opacity, the task is not to eliminate doubt, but to discipline it—distinguishing vigilance from paranoia, inquiry from ideology, and skepticism from cynicism. The sections that follow develop a typology designed to make these distinctions explicit and to clarify what is at stake when they collapse.

I. The Problem with the Word "Conspiracy"

The term *conspiracy theory* has become one of the most imprecise and rhetorically loaded labels in contemporary public discourse. It is routinely applied to claims that differ radically in evidentiary support, plausibility, and intent—collapsing documented coverups, reasonable suspicions, speculative hypotheses, and outright delusions into a single dismissive category. This conceptual flattening obscures meaningful distinctions and undermines serious analysis.

Historically, a conspiracy referred to coordinated action undertaken in secret—typically by multiple actors—for illicit or deceptive ends. By that definition, conspiracies are neither rare nor hypothetical. Governments, corporations, and political movements have repeatedly engaged in covert coordination later confirmed through declassified documents, investigative journalism, and whistleblower testimony.[1] Yet in contemporary usage, the phrase *conspiracy theory* has drifted from this descriptive meaning and now functions primarily as a pejorative—less an analytical category than a signal that a claim should not be taken seriously.

This rhetorical shift carries significant consequences. When the same label is applied to COINTELPRO and flat-Earth belief, or to legitimate questions about regulatory capture and claims of reptilian elites, the public is left without a vocabulary for distinguishing skepticism from fantasy. The result is epistemic confusion rather than clarity. Claims are rejected or accepted not on the basis of evidence, but on whether they trigger the stigma attached to the word itself.

More troublingly, *conspiracy theory* is often deployed as a tool of delegitimation. Rather than engaging the substance of a critique, institutions and media actors may dismiss it by association— implying irrationality, paranoia, or bad faith without addressing the evidence. This practice does not merely silence fringe beliefs; it can also suppress legitimate inquiry, particularly when questions challenge powerful interests or uncomfortable narratives.

The overuse of the label thus produces a paradox. By collapsing warranted suspicion and delusion into a single category, it weakens institutional credibility while strengthening conspiratorial worldviews. Individuals who see plausible concerns dismissed out of hand learn an unintended lesson: official denial is not a reliable signal of falsehood, but a reflex of power.[2]

The problem, then, is not simply that conspiracy beliefs exist, but that the language used to describe them lacks precision. Without a framework capable of differentiating among types of claims, public discourse oscillates between moral panic and epistemic nihilism. Everything becomes either obviously false or secretly true, with little room for disciplined uncertainty.

This chapter begins from a simple premise: not all conspiracies are created equal, and treating them as such is analytically lazy and politically counterproductive. To evaluate belief responsibly, we must move beyond the blunt instrument of stigmatizing labels and develop a vocabulary that distinguishes justified skepticism from corrosive paranoia. Only then can disbelief be addressed in ways that protect inquiry, reduce harm, and restore the possibility of trust.

II. Why a Spectrum Is Needed

Treating conspiracy belief as a binary—rational or irrational, true or false—fails to capture how disbelief actually operates in social and political life. Such binaries presume beliefs are static, when in reality they are contextual, contingent, and evolving. People arrive at conspiratorial interpretations through different pathways, under different conditions, and with varying degrees of justification. A framework that cannot register these differences will misdiagnose both belief and response.

A spectrum approach recognizes that conspiratorial thinking varies along multiple dimensions: evidentiary support, openness to revision, moral orientation, and susceptibility to harm. Some claims are grounded in documented facts and later vindicated by historical record. Others begin as reasonable suspicions in response to secrecy or inconsistency. Still others harden into ideological narratives that resist evidence altogether. Collapsing these forms into a single category obscures the boundary between warranted skepticism and corrosive belief.

The need for a spectrum is not merely analytical; it is ethical. When legitimate suspicion is treated as indistinguishable from delusion, institutions risk delegitimizing inquiry itself. Conversely, when all skepticism is indulged in the name of open-mindedness, harmful falsehoods gain space to metastasize. A spectrum allows us to hold both truths: that distrust can be justified, and that it can also become destructive.

A spectrum clarifies response. Documented conspiracies demand acknowledgment and reform. Reasonable suspicions require transparency and accountability. Coherent but unproven claims call for open inquiry and evidentiary rigor. Ideologically driven narratives demand challenge and contextualization. Delusional or weaponized beliefs require containment and harm reduction. Without such differentiation, responses default to blunt instruments—ridicule, censorship, or blanket debunking—that often exacerbate the very dynamics they seek to address.

The spectrum can be rendered more explicitly:

Type of Belief	Defining Features	Epistemic Status	Appropriate Response
Documented conspiracies	Verified covert coordination (e.g., COINTELPRO, Tuskegee)	Established	Acknowledgment, accountability, reform
Reasonable suspicions	Rooted in opacity, inconsistency, or past betrayal	Plausible, unconfirmed	Transparency, investigation, accountability
Unproven but coherent claims	Internally consistent; evidence incomplete or contested	Indeterminate	Open inquiry, evidentiary testing
Ideological narratives	Selective evidence; resistant to disconfirmation	Distorted	Challenge, contextualization, counter-evidence
Delusional or weaponized beliefs	Self-sealing, unfalsifiable, often mobilizing harm	Detached	Containment, harm reduction

A spectrum framework makes visible how beliefs move. Conspiracy beliefs are not fixed positions; they migrate over time. Institutional behavior plays a decisive role in this movement. Transparency, humility, and responsiveness can pull beliefs toward the center of the spectrum, where inquiry remains possible. Dismissal, secrecy, and contempt push beliefs outward, where they harden into self-sealing systems resistant to correction.

Understanding belief as mobile is essential for preventing escalation.[3]

Finally, a spectrum approach restores proportionality to public discourse. It allows us to distinguish between skepticism that strengthens democratic accountability and paranoia that corrodes it. It avoids false equivalence without reverting to panic. Most importantly, it reframes conspiracism not as defective cognition, but as a problem of epistemic governance—how societies manage doubt, disagreement, and uncertainty without collapsing trust or suppressing inquiry.[4]

For these reasons, a spectrum is not a concession to conspiratorial thinking. It is a corrective to analytical laziness. It provides a disciplined way to differentiate belief, assign responsibility, and respond proportionately—preserving space for legitimate skepticism while identifying when belief becomes dangerous.

III. The Conspiracy Spectrum: A Proposed Typology

To move beyond the conceptual confusion surrounding conspiratorial belief, this chapter proposes a five-part typology—outlined above as a spectrum—that differentiates forms of conspiracy thinking according to evidentiary support, epistemic posture, and potential for harm. These categories are not moral judgments. They are analytical tools designed to clarify how different kinds of belief function—and how institutions and societies should respond.

This typology is not a linear progression or a judgment of individual psychology. People may hold beliefs across different positions simultaneously, depending on context. Nor is movement along the spectrum inevitable: beliefs shift in response to evidence, institutional behavior, and social reinforcement. The spectrum describes epistemic posture —how beliefs relate to evidence—not moral character.

The spectrum is not morally neutral: movement outward is marked by declining evidentiary responsiveness, increasing insulation from corrective feedback, and greater potential for harm. While skepticism at the inner end can strengthen accountability, beliefs at the outer end resist revision and often justify exclusion, scapegoating, or institutional sabotage. The distinction is therefore not merely descriptive, but civic.

1. Documented Conspiracies (Confirmed)

At one end are documented conspiracies—covert actions later established through credible evidence such as declassified documents, judicial findings, investigative reporting, or whistleblower testimony. Examples include COINTELPRO, MKUltra, the Tuskegee syphilis study, and the tobacco industry's suppression of internal research.

These are not theories but historical facts, often revealed after prolonged denial. Their existence helps explain persistent skepticism toward authority: conspiracies are not aberrations, but recurring features of unaccountable power.

Appropriate response: acknowledgment, accountability, and institutional reform. Treating these cases as irrational belief erases legitimate grievance and further undermines trust.

2. Reasonable Suspicion (Justified Skepticism)

The next category consists of reasonable suspicion—skepticism grounded in observable incentives, documented behavior, or structural conflicts of interest, even when direct proof is incomplete. Examples include concerns about regulatory capture, corporate lobbying, intelligence manipulation, or government secrecy.

These suspicions do not assume omnipotent coordination or reject evidence in advance. They remain open to confirmation or refutation and often motivate legitimate demands for transparency. Many have historically proven well-founded.

Appropriate response: seriousness without validation, transparency without condescension, and accountability without dismissal. Treating reasonable suspicion as paranoia risks pushing it toward more extreme forms.

3. Coherent but Unproven Claims (Investigatory Conspiracies)

Further along are coherent but unproven claims—hypotheses proposing coordination or concealment without conclusive evidence. Examples include early speculation about the Epstein network, CIA involvement in coups prior to declassification, or early lab-leak hypotheses.

These claims occupy an unstable middle ground. They may be wrong or incomplete, but are not inherently irrational. Their defining feature is openness to evidence: they can be confirmed, refuted, or radicalized if inquiry is prematurely closed.

Appropriate response: open investigation, clear evidentiary standards, and resistance to both reflexive dismissal and credulous amplification. Premature certainty—either for or against—does epistemic harm.[5]

4. Ideologically Driven Narratives (Politicized Belief)

At this stage, conspiratorial belief becomes ideologically organized. Claims are selected and interpreted based on political identity rather than evidence. Examples include expansive "deep state" narratives, unsupported election fraud claims, or civilizational conspiracies such as the "Great Replacement."

These narratives retain surface plausibility but resist disconfirmation. Evidence is applied asymmetrically, and belief shifts from inquiry to mobilization.

Appropriate response: firm challenge, contextualization, and separation of grievance from factual claim. Ridicule entrenches identity; silence normalizes it.

5. Delusional or Harmful Paranoia (Pathological or Weaponized)

At the far end are delusional or weaponized belief systems—self-sealing, unfalsifiable, and often detached from reality. Examples include QAnon, flat-Earth cosmology, or claims involving non-human elites controlling global events.

These systems operate outside shared epistemic norms and are often amplified for political or economic gain. This category describes belief structures, not clinical diagnoses; adherents are typically embedded in reinforcing information environments. While not all are violent, these narratives can justify harassment, vigilantism, or institutional sabotage.

Appropriate response: containment, harm reduction, and disruption of amplification. Debate alone is insufficient.[6]

The Value of Differentiation

This typology does not excuse conspiratorial belief or deny its dangers. It clarifies that belief quality matters—and that institutional response shapes whether skepticism remains constructive or becomes corrosive. Treating all conspiratorial claims as equivalent collapses meaningful distinctions and accelerates epistemic escalation.

Understanding belief as a spectrum allows societies to protect legitimate inquiry while identifying when it becomes harmful. It restores proportionality to response and accountability to authority—both necessary for rebuilding trust under conditions of epistemic opacity.

IV. Borderlands: Where Beliefs Shift Along the Spectrum

Conspiracy beliefs do not remain fixed within a single category. They move—sometimes gradually, sometimes abruptly—across the spectrum in response to evidence, institutional behavior, and social reinforcement. These borderlands—where beliefs shift between justified skepticism and corrosive paranoia—are the most epistemically consequential terrain, and the point at which institutional response matters most.

Beliefs often begin as reasonable suspicion or investigatory inquiry, emerging in response to secrecy, inconsistency, or visible incentive misalignment. When institutions respond with transparency and procedural openness, such beliefs can stabilize or resolve. When they respond with dismissal, ridicule, or premature certainty, those same beliefs are pushed outward—toward ideological hardening and self-sealing logic.[7]

Recent history offers clear illustrations. Early discussion of a possible laboratory origin of COVID-19 was, at certain stages of the pandemic, publicly characterized as implausible or conspiratorial despite limited evidence and evolving uncertainty. As official positions shifted and investigation reopened, the claim moved back toward the center of the spectrum. The epistemic damage, however, was already done: early dismissal trained audiences to interpret institutional denial as reflexive rather than evidentiary. The issue was less the error than the asymmetry of response—public certainty asserted before evidentiary closure.[8]

Other cases demonstrate movement in the opposite direction. Claims surrounding the assassination of John F. Kennedy span nearly the entire spectrum. Some rest on declassified evidence and confirmed deception; others extend into unsupported speculation. Over time, partial disclosure and unresolved ambiguity have allowed legitimate questions to coexist with increasingly implausible claims—blurring distinctions institutions failed to clarify.

A similar pattern can be observed in responses to large-scale economic crises, particularly the 2008 financial collapse. Early public suspicion focused on concrete, verifiable dynamics: predatory lending, regulatory capture, and the moral hazard of institutions deemed "too big to fail." These concerns were grounded in documented misconduct and widely acknowledged failures of oversight. Yet as accountability remained limited and elite actors largely escaped consequence, legitimate skepticism drifted outward. Structural explanations, complex and procedural, gave way to personalized narratives of hidden coordination and intentional betrayal. Here, epistemic drift was driven not by misinformation, but by the prolonged absence of visible accountability.

More dangerous trajectories emerge when satire, speculation, or fringe belief is absorbed into moralized political identity. The evolution of "Pizzagate" illustrates how a claim can move rapidly from fringe rumor to mobilizing narrative. What began as online conjecture hardened through repetition, emotional reinforcement, and institutional silence into a perceived moral emergency—demonstrating how beliefs accelerate when grievance and identity override evidentiary restraint.[9]

The same belief can occupy different positions simultaneously, depending on context and actor. A question raised tentatively by an investigative journalist may function differently when amplified by partisan influencers or algorithmic systems. The epistemic status of a claim—how well it is supported and justified—is shaped not only by evidence, but by who advances it, how it circulates, and what incentives govern its amplification.

These borderlands reveal why binary approaches fail. Beliefs do not shift simply because they are true or false, but because epistemic environments reward certainty over caution, identity over inquiry, and allegiance over correction. Early institutional response often determines whether skepticism remains constructive or hardens into paranoia.

The question is not why people "fall" into conspiracism, but how beliefs are pushed there. When institutions foreclose inquiry, deny uncertainty, or weaponize dismissal, they accelerate drift. When they respond proportionately, they slow it.

The borderlands are therefore the most important site of intervention. Preventing destructive conspiracism does not begin at the extreme, where correction is least effective. It begins earlier—where doubt remains open, questions revisable, and trust not yet exhausted.

V. The Role of Institutions in Shaping the Spectrum

Institutions do not merely respond to conspiracy belief; they shape where it settles along the spectrum. When they violate the moral grammar described earlier—through defensiveness, selective disclosure, or refusal of answerability—they narrow the center and accelerate epistemic drift—the movement of beliefs away from evidence-responsive skepticism toward more rigid or self-sealing forms. Across the cases examined in this book, several institutional behaviors consistently push belief outward: asserting certainty where uncertainty exists; delaying or selectively disclosing information; failing to impose visible consequences for elite misconduct; conflating dissent with bad faith; and substituting ridicule for explanation. None require malicious intent to be damaging. Their cumulative effect is epistemic: they teach audiences that authority is more invested in managing perception than in sustaining credibility.

Through their communication practices and treatment of dissent, institutions can either stabilize skepticism within productive bounds or accelerate its drift toward paranoia. The difference lies less in what institutions know than in how they speak, explain, and correct.

Transparency plays a decisive role. When institutions disclose information proactively, acknowledge uncertainty, and explain the limits of their knowledge, they create conditions in which doubt can coexist with trust. Skepticism remains tethered to inquiry. By contrast, opacity—especially when paired with confident assertion—signals that information is being managed rather than shared. In such environments, suspicion is not irrational; it is adaptive.[10]

Accountability functions similarly. Institutions that admit error, correct publicly, and impose visible consequences slow belief migration toward ideological hardening. Where mistakes are concealed, responsibility deflected, or consequences delayed, belief moves outward. The issue is not fallibility—error is inevitable—but whether it is acknowledged or suppressed.

Equally important is the treatment of dissent. When institutions conflate questioning with bad faith, they collapse distinctions between inquiry and antagonism. Critics are recast as threats rather than participants. This pushes even moderate skepticism toward defensive identity, where belief becomes less about truth-seeking and more about self-protection. Ridicule is especially corrosive. It does not persuade; it signals that power prefers silence to explanation.[11]

Institutional inconsistency compounds these effects. Shifting narratives without acknowledgment, reversing guidance without explanation, or selectively enforcing standards erode credibility even when revised positions are substantively correct. Over time, audiences learn to treat institutional confidence as provisional and self-serving. Once this expectation takes hold, even accurate information struggles to persuade.

Institutions also shape the spectrum through what they reward. When media systems, regulators, or political actors incentivize certainty, loyalty, or emotional resonance over accuracy and humility, they distort the epistemic environment. Actors who simplify or moralize gain visibility, while those who qualify or explain appear evasive. Institutions that fail to counter these incentives inadvertently promote the escalation they later condemn.

The cumulative effect is epistemic drift. Beliefs that begin as reasonable questions migrate toward rigidity not because evidence demands it, but because institutional behavior forecloses the middle ground. The spectrum narrows, positions polarize, and institutions are left confronting extremes they helped produce.

Recognizing the institutional role does not absolve individuals of responsibility, nor deny the harms of conspiratorial thinking. It clarifies causality. Institutions possess disproportionate power to stabilize or destabilize public epistemology—the shared conditions through which societies determine what counts as credible knowledge. When exercised carelessly or defensively, that power becomes accelerant rather than corrective.

If conspiracism is to be addressed effectively, institutional reform must precede belief correction. Without restoring transparency, accountability, and epistemic respect—treating people as capable knowers whose questions deserve serious engagement—efforts to combat misinformation will continue to treat symptoms while reinforcing causes. The spectrum is not merely a map of belief; it is a mirror of institutional conduct.

VI. Preventing Spectrum Drift

Preventing legitimate skepticism from sliding into corrosive paranoia requires more than correcting false claims after they harden. It requires earlier intervention, while belief remains provisional and inquiry possible. Spectrum drift is not inevitable; it is shaped by institutional choices, communicative norms, and the incentives that govern public explanation.

The first safeguard is public inquiry without humiliation. Institutions must create visible channels through which questions can be asked, investigated, and answered without stigma. This does not mean validating every suspicion. It means responding proportionately by acknowledging uncertainty, explaining evidentiary limits, and distinguishing between unanswered questions and unfounded conclusions. When inquiry is treated as a threat, skepticism becomes defensive and identity-bound.[12]

Second, transparency must be procedural, not performative. Selective or defensive disclosure often worsens distrust. What stabilizes belief is not disclosure alone, but intelligibility: explanations that clarify how decisions are made, why tradeoffs exist, and where responsibility lies. Transparency that follows pressure or scandal signals concession rather than integrity—and accelerates drift.

Third, institutions must resist weaponizing debunking. Fact-checking is necessary, but when used as a rhetorical bludgeon—especially early in an evidentiary cycle—it can harden belief rather than correct it. Labeling claims "false" without explaining standards of evaluation, or dismissing uncertainty as malice, signals control rather than truth. Effective correction is dialogical, not declarative.[13]

Fourth, preventing drift requires addressing underlying grievances, not just surface beliefs. Conspiratorial narratives often attach to real experiences of harm, neglect, or exclusion. When institutions focus only on belief content, they leave the motivational structure of suspicion intact. Addressing inequality, regulatory failure, or institutional abuse does not eliminate conspiracism—but it deprives it of its most credible fuel.[14]

Fifth, incentive structures must be realigned. Media systems, political institutions, and professional norms often reward certainty, speed, and moral clarity over caution and revision. These incentives push both institutions and citizens toward extremes. Slowing the pace of authoritative claims, normalizing revision, and rewarding epistemic humility can widen the center of the spectrum.

Finally, preventing drift requires epistemic respect. This does not mean treating all beliefs as equal; it means treating belief holders as agents rather than problems. When institutions communicate with contempt, they invite it in return. When they communicate with clarity and restraint, they preserve the conditions under which trust can be rebuilt.

The goal is not to eliminate distrust—some distrust is justified—but to prevent it from hardening into self-sealing worldviews that reject correction. That work begins at the center of the spectrum—where doubt remains compatible with dialogue and skepticism still points toward accountability rather than despair.

Preventing spectrum drift is therefore less about controlling belief than about governing responsibly under uncertainty. Institutions that accept this responsibility can slow escalation, preserve inquiry, and reduce harm. Those that do not will discover that disbelief, once hardened, is far more difficult to contain than it would have been to engage.

Conclusion

Not all disbelief is dangerous, and not all conspiratorial belief is irrational. What matters is where skepticism falls along the spectrum, how it relates to evidence, and how it is shaped by institutional behavior. Treating conspiracy belief as a single phenomenon obscures these distinctions and invites responses that are either dismissive or indiscriminate—both of which deepen mistrust rather than resolve it.

Conspiratorial belief ranges from documented fact to delusional or weaponized paranoia, with intermediate forms differing in legitimacy, risk, and consequence. Recognizing this spectrum allows for proportional response: it protects justified skepticism from being pathologized while identifying the points at which belief becomes corrosive to democratic life.

Crucially, belief does not move along this spectrum in isolation. Institutions shape epistemic trajectories—how beliefs develop, shift, and harden over time—through how they handle uncertainty, dissent, accountability, and explanation. Transparency can stabilize doubt; ridicule can radicalize it. Early engagement can preserve inquiry; premature dismissal can harden belief into identity. The boundary between vigilance and paranoia is not fixed—it is continually produced through institutional conduct.

The central lesson is not simply about conspiracies, but about governance under conditions of uncertainty. Societies do not fail because people ask too many questions. They fail when institutions respond with opacity, defensiveness, or contempt. In such environments, skepticism does not disappear—it hardens into forms that reject correction altogether.

Understanding conspiracy belief as a spectrum restores analytical clarity. It allows us to distinguish inquiry from ideology, suspicion from delusion, and accountability from scapegoating. More importantly, it reframes the task ahead: not the eradication of doubt, but the cultivation of conditions under which doubt remains constructive.

Where conspiratorial thinking is often treated as a binary—rational or irrational, true or false—this framework instead captures its variation, movement, and dependence on institutional context.

The next chapter turns to how institutional drift and accountability vacuums further destabilize these conditions—and how they amplify the very dynamics this chapter has sought to clarify.

REFERENCES

[1] Kathryn S. Olmsted, *Real Enemies: Conspiracy Theories and American Democracy, World War I to 9/11* (Oxford University Press, 2009).

[2] Miranda Fricker, *Epistemic Injustice: Power and the Ethics of Knowing* (Oxford University Press, 2007).

[3] Jaron Harambam, *Contemporary Conspiracy Culture* (Routledge, 2020).

[4] Onora O'Neill, *A Question of Trust* (Cambridge University Press, 2002).

[5] Michael Butter, *The Nature of Conspiracy Theories* (Polity Press, 2020).

[6] Quassim Cassam, *Conspiracy Theories* (Polity Press, 2019).

[7] Harambam, *Contemporary Conspiracy Culture.*

[8] Zeynep Tufekci, "Why Did It Take So Long to Take the Lab Leak Theory Seriously?" *The New York Times*, June 4, 2021.

[9] Whitney Phillips, *This Is Why We Can't Have Nice Things* (MIT Press, 2018).

[10] O'Neill, *A Question of Trust.*

[11] Fricker, *Epistemic Injustice.*

[12] O'Neill, *A Question of Trust.*

[13] Stephan Lewandowsky et al., "Misinformation and Its Correction: Continued Influence and Successful Debiasing," *Psychological Science in the Public Interest* 13, no. 3 (2012).

[14] Mark Fenster, *Conspiracy Theories: Secrecy and Power in American Culture* (University of Minnesota Press, 2008).

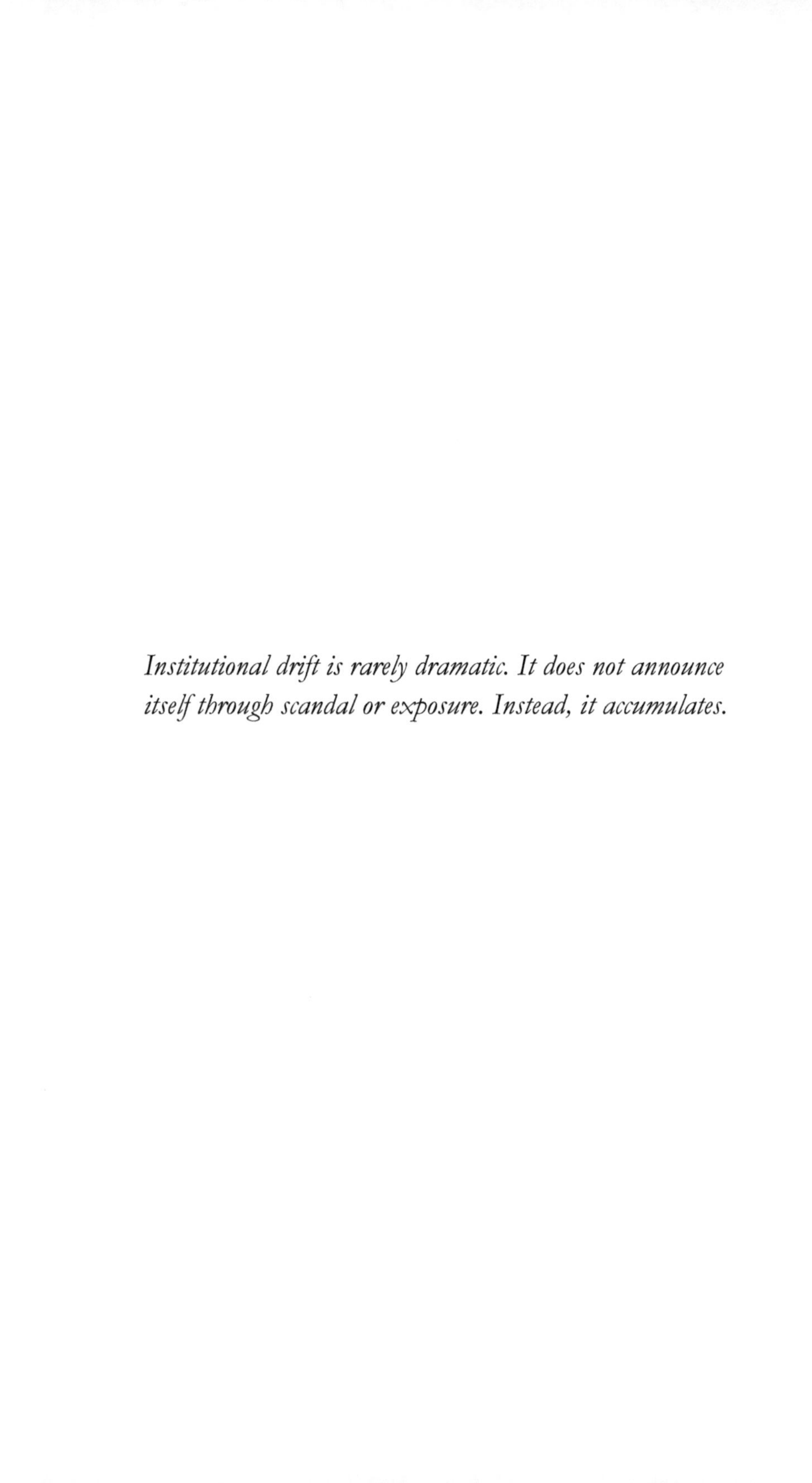

Institutional drift is rarely dramatic. It does not announce itself through scandal or exposure. Instead, it accumulates.

CHAPTER 9

Institutional Drift and Accountability Vacuums

How Policy Incoherence and
Bureaucratic Ambiguity Fuel Belief

Public mistrust is often attributed to secrecy, deception, or disinformation. Yet in many contemporary cases, distrust emerges not from what institutions hide, but from what they fail to account for— from inconsistency, ambiguity, and missing responsibility. Even when no single lie can be identified, belief erodes when institutions cannot explain themselves coherently.

this chapter shifts focus toward institutional behavior. Building on the global patterns identified in Chapter 6 and the epistemic spectrum developed in Chapter 7, it argues that conspiracy belief flourishes most readily in environments marked by institutional drift: the gradual erosion of purpose, coherence, and moral anchoring within organizations that continue to function procedurally but no longer communicate clear responsibility or intent. Institutions do not need to collapse to lose trust; they need only become opaque in their own logic.

Institutional drift is rarely dramatic. It does not announce itself through scandal or exposure. Instead, it accumulates through incremental misalignment— between stated mission and practice, justification and outcome, and authority and accountability. Policies change without explanation. Guidance shifts without acknowledgment. Errors are diffused across agencies, committees, and legal frameworks until no single actor appears responsible. Over time, the system continues to operate, but it no longer appears to mean what it claims.

The result is an accountability vacuum. When decisions produce harm or confusion and no one visibly answers for them, citizens are left without a credible account of cause and consequence. Apologies without reform, investigations without consequences, and explanations without ownership teach a subtle but powerful lesson: responsibility has become abstract. In such environments, people do not merely doubt specific claims; they begin to doubt whether the system itself is oriented toward truth or justice.

Crucially, accountability vacuums do not require malicious intent. They can arise from complexity, fragmentation, legal insulation, or risk-averse bureaucratic culture. Yet their epistemic effect is the same. Their impact reaches how people understand what is credible, who is responsible, and how truth is established. When authority cannot be located, explained, or challenged, uncertainty becomes personalized.. Citizens supply the coherence institutions fail to provide, often through conspiratorial narratives that restore intentionality, agency, and moral clarity where bureaucracy offers only process and deferral.

This chapter examines how institutional drift and accountability vacuums reshape the environment under which belief forms. It explores how contradictory messaging, bureaucratic diffusion of responsibility, and ethical erosion—rather than secrecy alone—fuel suspicion. It also considers the psychological consequences of prolonged exposure to incoherent authority: not paranoia, but institutional fatigue—a condition in which people cease to expect clarity, fairness, or moral direction from the systems that govern them.

The argument advanced here is not that institutions are uniquely deceptive, nor that conspiratorial belief is justified. It is that trust erodes when institutions lose the capacity to account for themselves in intelligible and morally grounded ways. Where explanation fails, alternative narratives take hold. Where responsibility is unclear, intent is inferred. And where systems drift without correction, belief migrates toward frameworks that promise coherence—even at the cost of accuracy.

By tracing the relationship between institutional drift and conspiratorial belief, this chapter prepares the ground for a central claim of this book: restoring trust is less a matter of persuading citizens than of rebuilding institutional legibility and accountability. Before asking why people believe what they do, we must first ask whether the institutions they are asked to trust still know—and can explain—what they are doing.

I. What Is Institutional Drift?

Institutional drift refers to the gradual erosion of purpose, coherence, and ethical grounding within organizations that continue to function formally but no longer operate in alignment with their stated mission or public justification. It is not a scandal or a sudden collapse. It is a slow misalignment between what institutions claim to do, what they actually do, and how their actions are experienced by the public.

Drift occurs when rules persist but meaning thins. Procedures are followed, offices remain staffed, and policies are issued, yet the rationale for decisions becomes opaque even to those charged with implementing them. Mission statements remain unchanged while behavior adapts to convenience, political pressure, or risk avoidance. Over time, institutions retain authority without retaining clarity.

Unlike corruption or conspiracy, institutional drift does not require bad faith. It can emerge from complexity, fragmentation, or bureaucratic accretion. Layers of oversight intended to ensure accountability may instead diffuse it. Legal safeguards designed to prevent abuse may simultaneously prevent responsibility. In such systems, no single actor appears culpable, even when outcomes are plainly harmful or incoherent.

This distinction matters. When institutions fail through deception, exposure can restore trust by reasserting standards and consequences. When they fail through drift, exposure often changes little. There is no decisive revelation, only a growing sense that the system no longer knows—or cannot explain—what it is doing. Authority becomes procedural rather than purposive.

From the public's perspective, institutional drift is experienced less as malice than as disorientation. Policies shift without explanation. Guidance changes without acknowledgment. Errors are reframed as misunderstandings, and responsibility is distributed so widely that it disappears. Even when individual decisions are defensible in isolation, their cumulative effect is incoherence. People encounter outcomes without intelligible causes.

A common illustration of this disorientation occurs when a high-profile investigation is announced with confidence, framed as a serious effort to determine responsibility, and then quietly shelved without clear resolution. Months pass. Updates stop. Findings are delayed, narrowed, or deferred to internal review. No formal conclusion is communicated, no accountable decision-maker identified, and no explanation offered beyond procedural language. Even if the investigation was constrained by legal limits or evidentiary gaps, the absence of a clear account leaves the public with an unresolved narrative gap. What was initially presented as a search for truth comes to resemble an exercise in containment. Drift is felt not because wrongdoing is proven, but because responsibility disappears.

This erosion has an epistemic dimension. Drift reshapes how people judge credibility, assign responsibility, and interpret official explanations. When institutions cannot articulate consistent reasons for their actions, citizens begin to treat explanations as provisional or strategic rather than truthful. Trust weakens not because lies are discovered, but because meaning is no longer stable.

Institutional drift is therefore a precursor to deeper legitimacy crises. It creates the conditions under which accountability vacuums form, moral confidence decays, and alternative narratives gain appeal. Institutions do not lose trust all at once; they lose it incrementally, as clarity gives way to ambiguity and purpose yields to process.

Understanding institutional drift is essential to understanding why conspiracy belief flourishes even in the absence of secrecy or coordinated deception. When institutions cannot account for themselves, people seek coherence elsewhere. The sections that follow examine how this drift produces accountability vacuums, contradictory messaging, and bureaucratic opacity—and why these conditions invite belief systems that promise intention where institutions offer only inertia.

II. Accountability Vacuums

Accountability vacuums arise when institutions produce decisions, failures, or harms without a visible locus of responsibility. No single actor appears answerable, no clear explanation is offered, and no corrective consequence follows. Authority remains intact, but accountability thins.

These vacuums are not created by secrecy alone. They often emerge in plain sight, through procedural diffusion. Investigations are transferred between agencies, narrowed in scope, delayed indefinitely, or concluded without public explanation. A widely recognizable example occurred after the 2008 global financial crisis. Regulatory failures were publicly acknowledged, major institutions received emergency support, and extensive reviews were conducted. Yet high-level executive accountability remained limited, and consequences appeared asymmetrical. Formal reports were issued and settlements negotiated, but for many citizens the absence of visible moral resolution reinforced the perception that responsibility had dissolved upward into systemic complexity. The issue was not the absence of process, but the absence of identifiable ownership.

From an institutional perspective, such diffusion may be defensible. Complex systems require coordination, legal caution, and risk management. Yet from the public's perspective, the effect is unmistakable. When no one can say who decided, why they decided, or what follows from failure, authority begins to feel unmoored from consequence. Even accurate explanations lose force when they arrive without ownership.

Accountability vacuums are especially corrosive because they sever the link between error and learning. In healthy institutions, mistakes prompt visible correction: acknowledgment, reform, or sanction. In vacuum conditions, error is absorbed rather than addressed. Apologies are issued without reform. Reviews are conducted without change. The signal received is not that institutions are imperfect, but that they are insulated.

This insulation alters public interpretation. When outcomes recur without accountability, citizens begin to suspect that explanations are performative rather than sincere. The absence of responsibility is read not as complexity, but as concealment. Importantly, this suspicion does not require belief in a coordinated conspiracy. It emerges from repeated exposure to systems that explain themselves procedurally while avoiding moral or causal clarity.

Over time, accountability vacuums reshape expectations. People stop anticipating resolution. Investigations are assumed to end quietly. Oversight is expected to be symbolic. Trust erodes not through revelation, but through repetition. The lesson absorbed is not "they lied," but "nothing ever comes of it."

In such environments, conspiracy narratives gain traction because they restore what institutions have lost: identifiable agents, intentional causality, and moral consequence. Where official processes offer only diffusion and deferral, alternative explanations supply coherence. The appeal lies not in their accuracy, but in their ability to answer questions institutions leave unresolved.

Accountability vacuums therefore do more than undermine confidence in specific decisions. They weaken faith in institutional purpose itself. When responsibility cannot be located, authority no longer appears answerable to truth or justice. Belief migrates accordingly—not because citizens reject evidence, but because the systems tasked with producing meaning no longer appear capable of doing so.

III. When Institutions Contradict Themselves

Few dynamics erode trust more reliably than institutional contradiction. When official statements, policies, or standards conflict without clear explanation, people begin to suspect that stated principles are instrumental rather than sincere. Even well-intentioned institutions can generate mistrust when their actions no longer align with their declared logic.

A common and widely recognizable example occurs when rules are announced as universal but applied selectively. Standards described as necessary for public safety, legal integrity, or ethical compliance are enforced rigorously against ordinary citizens while exceptions are quietly extended to powerful actors. When justification remains constant but application varies, motive is inferred. What may begin as pragmatic discretion is experienced as double standard.

Another familiar contradiction arises when guidance changes without acknowledgment. Policies are revised, thresholds adjusted, or recommendations reversed, yet institutions speak as though continuity remains intact. Prior certainty is replaced with new certainty, but the transition is not explained as learning or error correction. Audiences are left to reconcile conflicting messages on their own. Over time, explanation gives way to suspicion of intent.

Legal and regulatory inconsistency produces similar effects. Courts may articulate principles—equal treatment under the law, neutrality, proportionality—while issuing rulings that appear to contradict them in practice. Regulatory agencies may invoke consumer protection or market fairness while approving actions that benefit concentrated interests. Even when legal reasoning exists, the gap between principle and outcome becomes difficult for non-specialists to reconcile. As these gaps recur, explanations begin to sound hollow.

Contradictions are especially destabilizing when institutions appeal to expertise while ignoring its limits. Officials may assert that decisions are "evidence-based" or "settled," only to revise them later without accounting for the change. Expertise itself becomes suspect—not because it is flawed, but because it is presented as infallible and then quietly amended.[1] The problem is not revision; it is revision without narrative continuity.

From within institutions, such contradictions may reflect complexity, uncertainty, or changing conditions. From the public's perspective, they signal incoherence. When explanations shift while authority remains constant, people begin to question whether truth or convenience is driving decisions. The institution's internal logic is no longer legible from the outside.

Repeated contradiction teaches a specific lesson: that official rationales are provisional and strategic. Once this expectation takes hold, even consistent messaging is discounted. People no longer ask whether an explanation is correct, but whether it will soon be replaced. Trust erodes not because institutions change their minds, but because they do so without acknowledging how those changes occur.[2]

In such environments, conspiracy narratives gain appeal because they resolve contradiction through intentionality. Where institutions offer shifting explanations without ownership, conspiracies offer stable motives and hidden coherence. The move toward alternative explanation is not a leap into fantasy; it is a response to perceived logical failure. When institutions contradict themselves without explanation, they invite narratives that claim to explain what official accounts cannot.

IV. Bureaucracy and the Disappearance of Responsibility

Modern bureaucracy was originally justified as a moral achievement. It promised rule-bound governance over arbitrariness, procedure over whim, and impersonal fairness over personal favor. Decisions would be made according to publicly knowable standards, and authority exercised through offices rather than individuals. In theory, this structure was meant to preserve responsibility, not erase it—to ensure that power could be traced, reviewed, and corrected.

Yet in practice, contemporary bureaucratic systems often produce the opposite effect. Responsibility does not vanish through secrecy, but through diffusion. Decisions are fragmented across agencies, committees, compliance offices, legal counsel, and advisory bodies. Each actor performs a bounded role—often competently and in good faith—while the system as a whole becomes incapable of answering basic moral questions: Who decided? On what grounds? And who is answerable for the outcome?

This diffusion creates a distinctive form of opacity—one that does not rely on concealment. Files are available. Processes are documented. Procedures are followed. And yet responsibility cannot be located. When outcomes are harmful, contradictory, or unjust, citizens encounter not denial but deferral. Authority points sideways, upward, or backward in time. The result is confusion. Power is experienced as everywhere and nowhere at once.

Western political traditions have long tied legitimacy to answerability—the expectation that authority must give reasons for its decisions and stand behind them as intentional acts subject to judgment. Bureaucracy was meant to institutionalize this expectation. When it instead obscures agency, it undermines the very justification for its existence.

The language of modern administration accelerates this erosion. Decisions are framed as "process-driven," "policy-compliant," or "outcome-neutral." Failures become "lessons learned." Harms are "unintended consequences." Each phrase reduces moral clarity while preserving institutional insulation. No one lies, but no one answers. Over time, citizens learn that appeals to procedure substitute for explanations of purpose, and legality substitutes for legitimacy.

This dynamic is particularly corrosive because it transforms error into inevitability. When responsibility is diffused, mistakes are no longer framed as correctable choices, but as emergent properties of complex systems. Reform becomes abstract, perpetual, and deferred. The moral vocabulary of accountability—fault, responsibility, redress—gives way to managerial language focused on optimization rather than justice. Institutions continue to function, but they cease to feel morally present.

This erosion also reshapes civic expectations. Citizens stop asking who is accountable and begin asking who benefits. When no official account identifies agency, alternative narratives fill the void. Conspiratorial explanations gain traction not because people reject complexity, but because complexity has been used to evade responsibility. Intentionality is reintroduced precisely because official systems refuse to claim it.

Importantly, this erosion does not require authoritarianism. It flourishes within democracies committed to legality, professionalism, and procedural restraint, and is often justified in their name. Excessive risk aversion, legal insulation, and reputational management, each defensible in isolation, combine to produce institutions that are insulated from blame but stripped of moral authority. The system survives, but trust does not.

This is where institutional drift becomes civilizationally consequential. Western societies have long rested on the premise that power must be explainable to those subject to it. Bureaucratic responsibility was meant to make authority legible, not abstract. When institutions can no longer say "we decided, and here is why," they forfeit more than confidence. They forfeit their claim to govern in the name of a shared moral order.

The disappearance of responsibility thus marks a critical threshold. Beyond it, distrust no longer signals episodic failure; it signals a breakdown in the moral contract between institutions and the public. In such conditions, belief systems that reassert agency— however inaccurately—begin to feel more truthful than official accounts that refuse to locate it at all.

Understanding bureaucracy's role in dissolving responsibility is therefore essential to understanding why conspiratorial narratives feel compelling even in highly procedural, rule-bound societies. Where institutions speak only in systems and processes, people seek explanations that speak in motives and choices. The turn toward alternative narratives is not a rejection of governance—it is a demand that someone, somewhere, finally answer for it.

V. Moral Drift and Institutional Cynicism

Moral drift refers to the gradual loss of ethical orientation within institutions—the slow decoupling of decision-making from clearly articulated principles of purpose, obligation, and public good. Institutions shift from asking "What is right?" to asking "What is defensible?" The change is subtle, but its implications are profound. It is not primarily a matter of lying or corruption. More often, it reflects a shift in institutional self-understanding: from serving a defined moral mission to managing risk, reputation, and continuity. When this shift persists, cynicism becomes not merely a reaction to institutions, but a feature of how they operate.

Institutional cynicism should be understood as a learned posture, not an attitude of contempt. It emerges when organizations repeatedly encounter situations in which ethical clarity carries cost while ambiguity offers protection. Decisions framed in moral terms invite scrutiny, accountability, and consequence; those framed in technical or procedural language diffuse responsibility and reduce exposure. Institutions adapt accordingly. Moral claims are softened, deferred, or avoided.

This pattern is visible across the global cases examined earlier in this book. In different political systems, institutional actors learn that asserting strong ethical commitments—about truth, fairness, or accountability—creates vulnerability. In their place emerge flexible narratives that preserve authority while minimizing obligation. Cynicism here does not mean disbelief in values; it means treating them instrumentally. Principles are invoked when useful and set aside when inconvenient.

As moral drift advances, institutions increasingly speak in the language of inevitability rather than choice. Outcomes are attributed to structural necessity, legal constraint, geopolitical reality, or systemic complexity. Responsibility is relocated from decision-makers to abstract forces. This rhetorical shift trains both officials and the public to treat harm as unfortunate but unavoidable. Moral judgment gives way to managerial assessment.

For citizens, prolonged exposure to this posture is corrosive. When institutions consistently avoid moral ownership, people stop expecting it. Trust does not collapse in outrage; it erodes into resignation. The public becomes cynical not because it rejects ethical claims, but because such claims no longer appear to guide institutional behavior. Cynicism becomes a rational adaptation to inconsistency.

Importantly, this pattern is not confined to any one regime type. As Chapter 6 demonstrated, cynicism appears under populist governments, nationalist states, managed authoritarian systems, and fragmented liberal democracies alike. What differs is not its presence, but its function. In some contexts, it stabilizes power by encouraging disengagement. In others, it fuels oppositional narratives that seek moral clarity elsewhere. In all cases, it reflects the same underlying condition: institutions that no longer convincingly bind authority to ethical purpose.

Moral drift also reshapes how institutions respond to criticism. When ethical commitment weakens internally, critique is interpreted less as a call to accountability than as a threat to legitimacy. Defensive communication replaces explanation. Transparency is treated as exposure. The gap between institutional self-protection and public expectation widens, reinforcing the very cynicism institutions seek to contain.

The danger of institutional cynicism is not that it denies morality outright, but that it empties moral language of consequence. Values remain present in rhetoric but absent in decision-making. This hollowing effect is especially destabilizing in societies whose legitimacy has historically rested on the claim that power is exercised for reasons that can be explained, defended, and judged. When institutions no longer appear to believe in their own moral claims, citizens search for frameworks that do.

In this way, moral drift extends the trajectory established earlier. Where responsibility disappears and principles lose force, conspiratorial narratives gain plausibility—not because they are accurate, but because they restore moral intentionality. They name villains where institutions name processes. They assign blame where institutions assign inevitability. Cynicism toward official explanation thus becomes fertile ground for belief systems that promise ethical clarity, however distorted.

Understanding institutional cynicism as a product of moral drift is essential to diagnosing contemporary mistrust. It shows that cynicism is not merely a cultural mood or psychological condition, but a systemic response to institutions that no longer anchor authority in morally accountable choice.

VI. The Psychology of Institutional Fatigue

Institutional fatigue describes a condition in which citizens cease to expect clarity, accountability, or moral direction from the systems that govern them. It is not paranoia, apathy, or radicalization. It is exhaustion—produced by repeated encounters with institutions that function procedurally while failing to resolve, explain, or meaningfully correct themselves.

This fatigue accumulates through familiar experiences. People file complaints that disappear into automated systems and receive templated responses weeks later. Appeals are acknowledged but never resolved. Regulatory processes stretch on while outcomes remain unchanged. Investigations are announced, paused, reframed, and quietly closed. Individually minor, these encounters accumulate into a lesson: engagement rarely produces results.

Over time, citizens learn to conserve energy. They stop tracking explanations closely because explanations rarely settle anything. Official statements are read as provisional. Press conferences are treated as theater. The effort required to stay informed begins to outweigh the perceived benefit. This withdrawal is not irrational. It is a rational response to systems that demand attention without offering resolution.

Institutional fatigue is reinforced when effort and compliance appear disconnected from outcome. People follow rules meticulously while observing that outcomes vary regardless. They meet requirements, submit documentation, wait through delays—only to see similar cases resolved differently without explanation. When process does not reliably produce fairness or consistency, the meaning of participation erodes. Compliance becomes habit rather than belief.

Another source of fatigue arises from perpetual crisis framing. Institutions frequently communicate in emergency mode, demanding trust, sacrifice, or restraint in the face of urgency. Yet emergencies recur without closure. Temporary measures become permanent. Extraordinary authority is normalized without retrospective accounting. Citizens are asked to move on without understanding what was learned or changed. Over time, urgency loses credibility, and appeals to trust sound hollow.

Fatigue also emerges from language itself. Official communication increasingly relies on abstractions—stakeholders, frameworks, compliance, best practices—while avoiding concrete moral claims. When harm occurs, it is described in passive terms: systems failed, gaps were identified, processes will be reviewed. Such language may be legally prudent, but it is emotionally alienating. People do not hear recognition of their experience; they hear insulation.

The psychological effect of this pattern is not immediate distrust, but lowered expectation. Citizens stop anticipating explanation or redress and begin to assume that outcomes are detached from accountability. This shift is subtle but consequential. When institutions are no longer expected to make sense, alternative explanations become more attractive—not because they are extreme, but because they offer coherence where official narratives do not.

Importantly, institutional fatigue does not push people directly toward conspiracy belief. It weakens the ground on which institutional explanations stand. When trust is exhausted, people become more receptive to narratives that promise agency and motive. Belief migrates not through persuasion, but through resignation. People stop asking whether institutions are correct and start asking whether anyone is truly in charge.

This condition helps explain why conspiracy narratives often take hold among otherwise pragmatic, informed individuals. Fatigue reduces tolerance for ambiguity without resolution. It increases demand for explanations that feel complete, even if they are flawed. In this sense, institutional fatigue is not a cognitive failure; it is a psychological adaptation to prolonged exposure to incoherent authority.

Institutional fatigue marks a critical transition point. Beyond it, trust is no longer actively withheld—it is passively withdrawn. Rebuilding credibility becomes exponentially harder because the audience is no longer listening closely enough to be persuaded. At this stage, restoring trust requires more than accurate information. It requires restoring the expectation that institutions will account for themselves meaningfully and consistently.

Understanding institutional fatigue is therefore essential to understanding why belief systems that offer clarity, blame, and intentionality gain appeal in drifted systems. Fatigue does not create conspiracism, but it prepares the ground on which it flourishes.

VII. Conspiracy as a Substitute for Coherence

When institutions drift, contradict themselves, diffuse responsibility, and exhaust public patience, they leave behind an explanatory vacuum. Conspiracy narratives enter that space not because they are inherently persuasive, but because they perform a function institutions increasingly avoid: they make outcomes intelligible. They assign cause where bureaucracy offers process, motive where institutions offer inevitability, and responsibility where authority has diffused into systems.

This substitution often begins in mundane contexts. When a policy produces harm and no official explanation names a decision-maker, people infer intention. When an investigation ends without conclusion, they assume containment. When rules are enforced inconsistently, they suspect favoritism. These inferences do not initially require belief in hidden cabals or grand designs. They emerge from repeated exposure to unresolved contradiction and unanswered questions.

Conspiratorial narratives succeed because they restore agency. Where institutional language describes outcomes as emergent, accidental, or unavoidable, conspiracies insist that someone chose the result. Where officials speak in abstractions—frameworks, constraints, processes—conspiracies speak in actors, interests, and goals. Even when these attributions are inaccurate or exaggerated, they can feel more truthful than explanations that refuse to locate responsibility.

These narratives also restore moral clarity. Bureaucratic explanations are often neutral by design. They describe what happened without addressing whether it was right, fair, or just. For citizens experiencing loss, exclusion, or harm, such neutrality reads as indifference. Conspiracy narratives reintroduce moral structure by identifying villains, victims, and betrayal. They impose ethical order on experiences institutions have rendered opaque.

Importantly, conspiracy as substitute coherence does not require belief in totalizing systems. Many people express conspiratorial suspicion selectively and situationally. They may distrust pharmaceutical companies but not doctors, governments but not local officials, media but not specific journalists. What unites these suspicions is not ideology, but a search for explanations that align action with consequence.

This helps explain why conspiratorial belief often intensifies where institutions are most complex. The more fragmented decision-making becomes, the harder it is to narrate responsibility. The more legalistic communication grows, the less it satisfies demands for meaning. In such environments, explanations that simplify—even dangerously—outcompete those that defer indefinitely.

Conspiracy narratives also provide psychological relief from institutional fatigue. They offer closure where official processes remain open-ended and replace uncertainty with conviction. For individuals worn down by years of unresolved issues, shifting standards, and opaque authority, this closure can feel stabilizing rather than destabilizing. The cost—detachment from evidence—is often deferred in favor of immediate coherence.

None of this implies that conspiratorial explanations are correct or harmless. They frequently misidentify causes, scapegoat groups, and harden into self-sealing belief systems. But their appeal is inseparable from institutional failure. Where systems consistently account for themselves—naming errors, explaining tradeoffs, and accepting responsibility—conspiracy narratives struggle to gain traction. Where they do not, such narratives appear less as aberrations than as compensations.

Conspiracy belief, in this sense, is not the primary problem but a secondary adaptation. It fills the space left by institutions that no longer explain their actions in morally intelligible terms. Its persistence therefore tells us less about the psychology of citizens than about the condition of the systems that govern them. Institutional failure may explain the appeal of conspiratorial narratives, but it does not make them accurate diagnoses of reality.

This does not absolve conspiratorial thinking of its harms. It clarifies causality. Belief migrates toward coherence wherever official explanation retreats from it. If institutions wish to counter conspiratorial narratives, they must first reclaim the explanatory ground they have ceded—not by asserting authority more forcefully, but by making responsibility visible again.

Conclusion

Conspiracy belief does not flourish solely because institutions deceive or conceal. It flourishes when institutions fail to account for themselves—when responsibility is diffused, explanations contradict outcomes, and moral purpose gives way to procedural insulation. In such environments, distrust emerges not from a single lie, but from the cumulative experience of incoherence.

This chapter has argued that institutional drift erodes trust by separating authority from clarity and power from answerability. Accountability gaps, bureaucratic diffusion, and moral drift weaken the link between decision and consequence, leaving citizens without a credible account of cause and responsibility. Over time, this produces institutional fatigue: a rational withdrawal of expectation that systems will explain themselves meaningfully or correct their failures.

Where institutions no longer provide coherence, alternative narratives step in. Conspiracy theories persist not because they are accurate, but because they restore agency, moral clarity, and intentionality where official explanations have become abstract or evasive. They function as compensatory frameworks—attempts to make sense of power when institutions no longer do.

The erosion of trust described here is not primarily a problem of belief, misinformation, or irrationality. It is a problem of governance under conditions of drift. When institutions cannot say who decided, why they decided, and what follows from error, they forfeit more than credibility. They forfeit their claim to be morally intelligible to those they govern.

Understanding conspiracy belief as a secondary adaptation to institutional incoherence reframes the challenge ahead. The task is not merely to correct false narratives, but to restore the conditions under which authoritative explanations can compete with them. Before trust can be rebuilt, institutions must recover the capacity to explain themselves clearly and with visible responsibility.

This recovery requires more than improved messaging. It requires structural change: reconnecting authority to consequence and policy to intelligible purpose. Institutions must narrow accountability gaps, restore visible ownership of error, and adopt communicative norms that acknowledge uncertainty without surrendering coherence.

The next chapter turns to these questions directly, shifting from diagnosis to design. If institutional drift and accountability vacuums drive epistemic fracture, the remedy is not better persuasion but the reconstruction of the shared civic infrastructure through which claims are made legible, contested, corrected, and owned—in other words, the rebuilding of an epistemic commons, a shared space where information and explanation can be trusted, tested, and publicly understood.

REFERENCES

[1] Sheila Jasanoff, *The Fifth Branch: Science Advisers as Policymakers* (Harvard University Press, 1990).

[2] Tom R. Tyler, *Why People Obey the Law* (Princeton University Press, 2006).

CHAPTER 10

Rebuilding the Epistemic Commons

Towards New Civic Infrastructures of Transparency and Repair

The preceding chapters have shown that distrust does not arise at the margins, nor is conspiratorial belief simply an error to be corrected. It emerges where authority no longer explains itself coherently or answers for its consequences. Diagnosis, however, is not enough. If mistrust is produced by opacity, contradiction, and diffused responsibility, repair must rebuild the conditions under which authority becomes legible again.

This chapter shifts from explanation to reconstruction. Its aim is not to persuade people to trust institutions as they are, but to ask what kinds of institutions are worthy of trust. Trust cannot be restored through messaging, enforcement, or appeals to expertise alone. It must be rebuilt through visible practices of transparency, participation, accountability, and moral clarity.

At the center of this effort lies the epistemic commons: the shared social space in which knowledge is generated, evaluated, and contested. This commons spans journalism, science, education, public institutions, and emerging civic technologies. It is the connective infrastructure through which societies determine what counts as credible, how disagreement is adjudicated, and who is answerable when claims fail. When it functions, truth remains a public good. When it degrades, truth fragments into private possession, partisan weapon, or algorithmic byproduct.

This is not a call to return to a lost golden age. The epistemic commons has always been partial, uneven, and contested. But it has, at times, functioned with greater coherence than it does today—and those conditions can be rebuilt and improved.

The crisis examined in this book is, at its core, a crisis of this commons. Institutions have grown opaque in their reasoning, defensive in their communication, and insulated from consequence, while digital systems have amplified noise and weakened shared reference points. Citizens are increasingly asked to accept conclusions without access to process, to trust expertise without visibility, and to defer judgment without accountability. Under such conditions, skepticism is not a pathology—it is a rational response to exclusion from meaning-making.

Rebuilding the epistemic commons therefore requires more than defending facts against falsehood. It requires restoring the civic infrastructures through which people can see how knowledge is produced, participate in its evaluation, and hold authorities accountable. This chapter does not propose a single blueprint. Instead, it outlines principles, reforms, and practices aimed at repairing the conditions under which shared reality becomes possible.

The task ahead is difficult but not utopian. Societies do not need perfect institutions; they need institutions that can explain themselves, admit error, and remain answerable to those they govern. The sections that follow begin by clarifying the epistemic commons, then turn to the principles and practices required to rebuild it in an age of fragmentation, fatigue, and legitimate distrust.

I. What Is the Epistemic Commons?

The epistemic commons refers to the shared social infrastructure through which knowledge is produced, vetted, and circulated within a society. It is not a single institution or authority, but an ecosystem composed of multiple actors and practices: journalism, scientific research, education, courts, public agencies, civic forums, and increasingly, digital platforms that mediate access to information. Together, these form the conditions that allow people to ask not only what is true, but how truth is established.

Like any commons, the epistemic commons depends on maintenance, boundaries, and stewardship. It requires norms of evidence, transparency in reasoning, mechanisms of correction, and shared expectations of accountability. When these conditions hold, disagreement remains productive rather than corrosive. People may dispute conclusions, but retain confidence in the processes that generate them. Authority remains contestable, but not arbitrary.

The epistemic commons has never been fully inclusive or stable. In earlier periods—particularly before the fragmentation of the digital, networked information environment—shared institutions such as broadcast media, print journalism, and professionalized expertise provided more coherent, if imperfect, mechanisms for establishing and contesting truth. These systems often excluded marginalized voices and concentrated interpretive authority, yet they sustained a more visible and widely shared framework for evaluating claims. The current crisis is not the loss of a perfect system, but the erosion of even this partial coherence.

When the epistemic commons degrades, inequality deepens. Some actors retain access to high-quality information, expert networks, and interpretive tools, while others navigate fragmented, algorithmically distorted environments. Truth becomes asymmetrically distributed. Those without access to institutional reasoning are asked to accept outcomes they cannot evaluate, creating fertile ground for suspicion. The issue is not ignorance, but exclusion from epistemic participation.

The collapse of the epistemic commons is often mistaken for a crisis of belief. In reality, it is a crisis of infrastructure. Institutions continue to generate claims, but no longer provide visibility into how those claims are formed. Corrections occur without narrative continuity. Expertise is asserted without reciprocal explanation. Over time, the public space in which knowledge can be collectively assessed erodes, replaced by parallel systems of interpretation that do not share standards or arbiters.

Understanding the epistemic commons in this way reframes the challenge of contemporary mistrust. The problem is not simply that falsehoods circulate more easily, but that the shared mechanisms for distinguishing truth from error have weakened. When people cannot see how decisions are made, how evidence is weighed, or how responsibility is assigned, they are effectively removed from the commons.

Rebuilding the epistemic commons therefore means restoring access to process, not merely access to conclusions. It requires institutions that make their reasoning visible, invite participation where appropriate, and remain answerable when they fail. Without such reconstruction, appeals to trust will continue to ring hollow. With it, trust can once again emerge as a byproduct of shared understanding rather than a demand imposed from above.

II. Trust Cannot Be Demanded—It Must Be Deserved

Across contemporary institutions, trust is increasingly treated as a communications problem. When confidence erodes, the default response is to refine messaging, streamline narratives, or amplify authoritative assertion. Campaigns are launched to "restore trust," experts are elevated to reassure, and dissent is framed as misunderstanding or bad faith. This approach reverses the relationship between trust and authority. Trust is not a prerequisite for legitimacy; it is a consequence of it.[1]

Trust does not arise because institutions ask for it. It arises because they demonstrate trustworthiness through visible practice. When this distinction is ignored, belief is treated as an obligation rather than an earned outcome. Citizens are expected to comply first and understand later—if at all. Under conditions of opacity and drift, this expectation is not merely unrealistic; it is destabilizing.

The difference between trust and trustworthiness is not semantic. Trust is a subjective posture held by citizens. Trustworthiness is a property of systems that can be observed in practice: whether they explain their reasoning, acknowledge uncertainty, admit error, and impose consequences when they fail. Trust can be withdrawn without warning. Trustworthiness must be built deliberately. When these categories collapse, compliance is mistaken for confidence and silence for assent.

This confusion has predictable effects. Public relations replaces explanation. Fact-checking substitutes for accountability. Expertise is asserted without visibility into process. Conclusions are defended while deliberation, tradeoffs, and internal disagreement remain obscured. The public is asked to accept outcomes without access to the reasoning that produced them. This is not how trust is generated. It is how suspicion is rationalized.

Citizens do not primarily demand reassurance. They demand explanation. They want to know how decisions were made, what constraints were present, which uncertainties remain unresolved, and who bears responsibility when outcomes cause harm. When these questions are met with messaging rather than explanation, confidence erodes even if the underlying facts are accurate. Trust fails not because information is wrong, but because authority is unaccountable.

The widespread reliance on fact correction illustrates this failure. Correcting false claims is necessary, but correction alone cannot substitute for credibility. When institutions fact-check assertions without addressing their own role in producing confusion, delay, or contradiction, they appear defensive rather than transparent. Truth presented without accountability reads as enforcement, not explanation. Over time, even accurate correction is discounted because it arrives without visible ownership of prior error.

Appeals to expertise can fail in similar ways. Expertise is essential in complex societies, but it does not function independently of process. When expert conclusions are presented as settled without showing how dissent was weighed, how uncertainty was managed, or how revision will occur, expertise becomes performative.[2] Authority is asserted rather than demonstrated. In such environments, skepticism toward experts does not signal anti-intellectualism. It reflects exclusion from epistemic participation: being denied access not just to conclusions, but to the processes through which knowledge is produced, evaluated, and contested.

This dynamic intensifies when doubt is met with moralization. Framing skepticism as irresponsibility, ignorance, or threat does not restore trust; it accelerates withdrawal. It teaches citizens that questioning is unwelcome and that authority prefers compliance to understanding. Once that lesson is learned, distrust becomes anticipatory.[3] People no longer wait to be misled; they assume opacity in advance.

The result is a vicious cycle. As trust declines, messaging intensifies. As messaging intensifies, credibility erodes further. Each side misdiagnoses the other. Institutions interpret skepticism as irrational hostility; citizens interpret reassurance as narrative control. What is lost is the middle ground where explanation, accountability, and mutual recognition might occur.

Reversing this cycle requires abandoning the demand for trust altogether. Institutions cannot be believed into legitimacy; they must be designed so that credibility emerges from practice rather than assertion.[4] This is not a matter of tone or virtue, but of structure. Trustworthiness must be built into how institutions operate, communicate, and correct themselves—before trust can reasonably follow.

The sections that follow treat trustworthiness as a design problem rather than a moral appeal. They outline the principles by which institutions can make their reasoning visible, their accountability legible, and their authority answerable. Only under such conditions can trust reemerge—not as obedience, but as a rational response to institutions that once again earn it.

III. Design Principles for Epistemic Repair

The task of rebuilding the epistemic commons is not a matter of persuading citizens to believe more readily, nor of suppressing disagreement more effectively. It is a matter of institutional design. If trust is to reemerge as a rational response rather than a coerced posture, institutions must be structured to make credibility visible, accountability legible, and reasoning accessible. The principles that follow are not policy prescriptions. They are normative design criteria—conditions that trustworthy institutions must satisfy regardless of domain.

These principles assume pluralism, contestation, and uncertainty as permanent features of democratic life. Their purpose is not to eliminate doubt, but to discipline it by restoring shared processes through which claims can be evaluated and authority can be questioned without collapse.

Principle 1: Transparency as Default

Transparency is not a concession; it is a precondition of legitimacy. When disclosure occurs only after leaks, litigation, or scandal, it signals damage control rather than integrity. By then, trust has already eroded.

Transparency by default means making reasoning visible before outcomes harden—including tradeoffs, uncertainty, and internal disagreement. It does not eliminate confidentiality, but it reverses the burden: institutions must justify secrecy.

A partial model can be seen in the U.S. Federal Reserve's evolution since the 1990s. Once highly opaque, it now publishes meeting minutes, economic projections, and dissenting votes. While far from perfect, this shift has made monetary policy more legible and reduced the need for speculative interpretation of intent.

Principle 2: Participation in Knowing

Trust increases when people can see how conclusions are reached—even when they disagree with them. Participation does not mean crowd-sourced truth or populist veto. It means structured visibility into knowledge-making.

Modern expertise is often necessary but opaque. When people are excluded from how decisions are formed, they infer hidden motives. Participation addresses this not by replacing expertise, but by making it inspectable.

Examples include citizen science initiatives and deliberative civic forums such as Oregon's Citizens' Initiative Review. In these processes, randomly selected citizens engage expert testimony, question assumptions, and produce publicly accessible reasoning about complex policy questions. Participants do not replace expertise; they make its operation visible. The result is not unanimity, but legitimacy.

Participation, at its core, restores shared ownership of process, even when outcomes remain contested.

Principle 3: Accountability That produces Consequence

Acknowledgment without consequence is not accountability—it is performance. When errors lead only to reports, apologies, or procedural review, institutions teach the public that failure carries no cost.

Accountability requires visible linkage between action and outcome: investigation, correction, and, where warranted, sanction. These responses must be intelligible, not buried in legal or administrative abstraction.

Post-Watergate reforms in the United States offer a partial example. Congressional investigations, resignations, and legal consequences established a visible chain between wrongdoing and accountability. The lesson was not that institutions are flawless, but that they are capable of self-correction.

Where consequence is absent, suspicion fills the gap.

Principle 4: Coherent Explanation with Moral Integrity

Institutions do not operate only through procedures—they operate through explanations. When decisions are technically precise but morally opaque, credibility erodes.

Coherence requires answering two questions: how was this decided, and why does it matter? Avoiding the second in the name of neutrality often produces the opposite effect—decisions appear evasive rather than impartial.

During the Cuban Missile Crisis, the Kennedy administration combined strategic secrecy with clear public reasoning about risk, stakes, and intent. The result was not full transparency, but intelligibility. Citizens could understand the logic of action, even under uncertainty.

Moral clarity does not mean certainty or moralizing. It means making values visible and consistent with action. When institutions fail to do this, people seek coherence elsewhere—often in narratives that supply intention where official accounts do not.

IV. From Principles to Practice: Institutional Reforms

The principles outlined above do not prescribe a single institutional model. They define criteria by which reforms can be judged: whether they make reasoning visible, accountability legible, and authority answerable. The domains below are therefore illustrative rather than exhaustive. Their purpose is not to offer uniform solutions, but to show that epistemic repair is possible in practice rather than merely in theory. This argument draws on work such as Elinor Ostrom's analysis of how shared resources can be governed through transparent rules, distributed oversight, and accountable participation.[5]

Media and Information Systems

Media institutions occupy a central position in the epistemic commons, yet they operate under pressures that reward speed, outrage, and alignment over explanation and verification. Repair does not require restoring a unified authority, but reinforcing functions that markets alone do not sustain.

One such function is investigative journalism. Public-interest funding through independent foundations, public media institutions, or protected endowments can reduce dependence on attention-driven revenue models. When journalism is tied to virality, explanation is displaced by provocation. Organizations such as

ProPublica (a U.S.-based nonprofit newsroom dedicated to long-form investigative reporting) demonstrate how alternative funding models can sustain work that prioritizes verification over immediacy.

Algorithmic mediation presents a newer challenge. Digital platforms now shape what information is seen and amplified, yet the criteria governing visibility remain opaque. Requiring auditability does not mean controlling content; it means making ranking and amplification systems subject to public scrutiny. Without such visibility, users infer intent where process is hidden, a dynamic that accelerates suspicion regardless of actual coordination.

Decentralized verification offers a partial counterbalance. Collaborative models such as the International Consortium of Investigative Journalists (ICIJ) distribute investigative work across independent actors operating under shared standards. This reduces reliance on single institutional authorities and strengthens credibility through cross-verification.

The more fundamental reform, however, is structural clarity. Media systems increasingly blur the boundaries between reporting, opinion, and institutional messaging—especially in moments of crisis. When these functions collapse into one another, audiences cannot distinguish evidence from interpretation or analysis from advocacy. The result is confusion about what is being claimed and on what basis.

Restoring these distinctions is therefore essential. Reporting establishes facts, opinion interprets them, and institutional messaging advances positions. When these roles remain legible, disagreement can persist without undermining confidence in the underlying information. When they do not, even accurate reporting is received as persuasion, and trust erodes accordingly.

Education

Education systems play a long-term but decisive role in shaping how citizens relate to knowledge, authority, and uncertainty—and thus in enabling epistemic repair. But epistemic repair here does not mean teaching what to believe; it means restoring the capacity of individuals to understand how knowledge is formed, challenged, and corrected, and to situate claims within processes of evidence, debate, and accountability.

This requires treating epistemic literacy as a core civic competency: the ability to evaluate how claims are made, what evidence supports them, how uncertainty is handled, and who is responsible when they fail. Students should learn not only how knowledge is produced—through method, evidence, and critique— but also how it breaks down.

Historical cases such as the Tuskegee syphilis study or the delayed recognition of tobacco's health risks demonstrate that institutions can be wrong, deceptive, or slow to correct themselves. Encountering such cases alongside examples of successful inquiry grounds trust in realism rather than idealization.

Including institutional failure alongside civic ideals is essential. When education presents institutions only in aspirational terms, later revelations of error register as moral shock rather than historical continuity. By contrast, acknowledging past abuses, exclusions, and blind spots prepares citizens to evaluate authority without either naïveté or nihilism. Skepticism becomes compatible with commitment rather than opposed to it.[6]

Education must also normalize uncertainty as a feature of knowledge rather than a failure of it. Students trained to expect certainty from authority are more likely to interpret revision as deception. Those who understand uncertainty as inherent to inquiry are better equipped to navigate changing evidence without assuming bad faith.

In this sense, epistemic literacy functions as inoculation against both blind trust and corrosive distrust: it equips citizens not simply to receive knowledge, but to interpret it—within processes, limits, and systems of accountability.

Government and Public Institutions

Nowhere is epistemic repair more consequential—or more difficult—than in government and public administration. These institutions exercise coercive authority and produce high-stakes outcomes, yet often do so through processes that remain opaque even to those subject to them.

One of the clearest existing models of epistemic accountability is the system of inspectors general (IGs) within the U.S. federal government. Established to provide independent oversight within executive agencies, IGs are empowered to audit programs, investigate misconduct, access internal records, and report findings publicly—often without prior approval from the institutions they oversee. Crucially, their authority is not merely advisory. When functioning properly, IG offices combine independence, investigative capacity, and public reporting in ways that make institutional behavior visible and contestable. High-profile investigations—such as the Department of Justice Inspector General's reports on FBI conduct or the Department of Defense IG's audits of wartime contracting—have demonstrated how internal oversight, when structurally protected, can surface failures that would otherwise remain obscured.

The significance of this model lies in its structure. Oversight is embedded within institutions but insulated from their immediate control. It has access to information, the authority to investigate, and the obligation to explain its findings publicly. Where these conditions hold, accountability becomes legible. Where they are weakened—through political interference, resource constraints, or limits on jurisdiction—credibility erodes accordingly.

A second reform domain involves extending this logic beyond existing oversight mechanisms. Independent review bodies— whether civilian oversight boards, regulatory auditors, or hybrid public-interest commissions—must be granted not only visibility but consequence. Oversight that cannot act remains performative. Oversight that can investigate, compel disclosure, and trigger reform interrupts accountability vacuums before they harden into cynicism.

Targeted transparency offers a complementary approach. Rather than attempting total openness—which can be impractical and counterproductive—institutions can designate specific domains for heightened visibility. Lobbyist registries, enforcement decision logs, and body-camera archives illustrate how traceability constrains abuse and clarifies responsibility. When consistently maintained, such measures reduce the need for speculation by making institutional action observable.

Finally, epistemic repair requires explicit ownership of decisions. "Explain your vote" or "explain your decision" requirements compel officials to articulate not only what they decided, but why. This practice—long embedded in judicial opinions and increasingly expected in regulatory decision-making—anchors authority in reason-giving rather than position. Over time, it reinforces the expectation that power must justify itself in intelligible terms.[7]

Taken together, these reforms do not promise consensus or certainty. They offer something more durable: institutions that can be questioned without collapse, corrected without denial, and trusted without illusion. In an environment defined by fatigue and fragmentation, that standard is not minimal—it is transformative.

V. Rebuilding Through Relational Repair

Epistemic repair is not only structural; it is also relational. Institutions do not interact with abstract publics, but with people—people who remember how they were treated during moments of uncertainty, error, and harm. Even well-designed systems lose credibility when their human interfaces communicate distance, defensiveness, or contempt. Conversely, institutions that demonstrate relational competence can retain legitimacy even amid disagreement and failure.

Trust begins with being heard. Listening does not mean agreement or validation of every claim. It means recognizing concerns as intelligible rather than dismissing them as noise or threat. When institutions respond directly to questions, engage critics without caricature, and permit dissent without penalty, they signal epistemic respect. This does not eliminate conflict, but it prevents skepticism from hardening into alienation.

How institutions handle error is equally decisive. Credibility depends less on avoiding mistakes than on how they are acknowledged. Admission paired with explanation signals learning; denial signals self-protection. Institutions that consistently acknowledge error strengthen authority by anchoring it in honesty rather than infallibility.[8]

What follows error matters as much as the admission itself. Institutions often engage intensely during crisis and then withdraw once attention fades. This pattern is experienced not as resolution, but as abandonment. Sustained presence—through follow-up communication, continued engagement, and visible reform—signals that harm was taken seriously. Trust accumulates through continuity, not isolated gestures.

Recognition of harm is central to this process. Institutions frequently acknowledge error in technical terms while avoiding its lived impact. Yet for those affected, harm is not procedural; it is experiential. Naming harm does not require accepting every claim as dispositive, but it does require acknowledging that institutional actions have human consequences. Where harm is minimized or ignored, distrust becomes moral rather than epistemic.

The treatment of dissent further shapes this environment. When critics are treated as enemies or pathologies, dissent becomes identity-bound and self-reinforcing. When dissent is engaged seriously—even when rejected—it remains connected to shared standards of reasoning. The difference determines whether disagreement remains productive or becomes corrosive.

Relational repair, however, has clear limits. Listening without reform becomes performative. Apology without consequence becomes hollow. Engagement without accountability becomes exhaustion. When structural opacity, accountability vacuums, or moral drift persist, relational gestures are eventually interpreted as manipulation rather than care.

Relational repair therefore functions as a multiplier, not a foundation. It amplifies the credibility of institutions that already demonstrate transparency, accountability, and moral coherence. Where those conditions are absent, it may delay distrust but cannot prevent it. Where they are present, relational competence allows trust to accumulate gradually, even under strain.

VI. Reclaiming the Public Sphere

Rebuilding the epistemic commons ultimately requires reclaiming the public sphere itself. Knowledge cannot function as a shared civic resource when governed exclusively by market incentives or state authority. It must be sustained through shared norms, transparent processes, and plural oversight if it is to remain both credible and free.

Two forms of capture threaten this possibility. The first is corporate. Contemporary information environments are structured by attention economies that reward engagement over explanation and certainty over nuance. Platform incentives privilege reaction over deliberation, amplifying outrage while penalizing uncertainty. In such environments, truth is evaluated less for accuracy than for virality.

This system also obscures responsibility. Decisions about visibility and amplification are governed by proprietary mechanisms shielded from public scrutiny. When influence is exercised without transparency, citizens infer motive where process is invisible. Suspicion arises not because coordination is proven, but because authority is unaccountable.[9]

The second danger is state overreach. In response to fragmentation and misinformation, governments increasingly frame epistemic governance as a matter of security—justifying censorship or expanding control over speech in the name of public safety. While such interventions may aim to prevent harm, authority grounded in coercion undermines its own legitimacy. When states position themselves as arbiters of truth rather than guarantors of fair process, dissent is recast as threat and accountability gives way to enforcement.[10]

Reclaiming the public sphere requires resisting both forms of capture. Epistemic authority cannot be monopolized—by markets or by states—without eroding trust. It must instead be distributed, transparent, and contestable.

Several existing models illustrate this possibility. Wikipedia operates through participatory verification rather than centralized assertion.[11] Its credibility derives not from infallibility, but from visible process: open editing, documented disputes, and iterative correction. Authority remains provisional, yet collectively sustained—even as the platform continues to face well-documented challenges around bias, uneven participation, and content reliability.

Open science platforms offer a parallel model. By emphasizing open data, pre-registration, and transparent peer review, they shift authority away from prestige and toward reproducibility. Knowledge remains contestable, but the grounds of contestation are publicly accessible.

Truth and reconciliation forums demonstrate the moral dimension of epistemic repair. By creating shared records of harm and responsibility, they enable societies to move forward without enforced amnesia. Their legitimacy derives not from coercion, but from participation and acknowledgment.[12]

These models are not uniform or universally transferable. Their significance lies in what they share: public governance of knowledge through transparency, participation, and institutional humility. They show that shared reality can be sustained without demanding belief or enforcing consensus.

Reclaiming the public sphere is therefore not about restoring consensus, but restoring conditions under which disagreement remains intelligible and truth remains a public good. Without such conditions, distrust becomes corrosive and belief migrates toward systems that promise certainty at the cost of freedom. With them, skepticism can function as a civic resource rather than a destabilizing force.

VII. A New Ethos: Epistemic Humility and Moral Clarity

Rebuilding the epistemic commons ultimately requires more than new structures or improved processes. It requires a shift in institutional ethos—a change in how authority understands its relationship to knowledge, uncertainty, and responsibility. Without such a shift, reforms risk becoming procedural veneers layered over the same credibility failures that produced distrust.

Epistemic humility is central to this transformation. Institutions must be willing to acknowledge what they do not know, what remains uncertain, and where evidence is incomplete. This is not a concession of weakness, but a recognition of the limits inherent in complex and contested realities. When provisional knowledge is presented as settled fact, revision invites backlash. When uncertainty is acknowledged openly, revision becomes intelligible rather than destabilizing.

Humility also requires making knowledge production visible. Conclusions that appear without method are experienced as decrees rather than judgments. By contrast, institutions that render their processes legible—how evidence is gathered, how disagreement is handled, how revision occurs—invite citizens into the work of knowing, even when they lack technical expertise. What matters is not mastery, but access to reasoning.

At the same time, humility must not collapse into relativism. Acknowledging uncertainty does not mean treating all claims as equal or all perspectives as equally grounded. Institutions retain a responsibility to distinguish between evidence-based conclusions and speculation, between disagreement and disinformation, and between inquiry and ideology. Epistemic humility disciplines certainty; it does not abandon standards.[13]

Moral clarity is the necessary complement. Institutions must be able to explain not only how decisions are made, but why they matter. Decisions are never purely technical; they reflect judgments about risk, harm, fairness, and responsibility. When these judgments are hidden behind neutral or technocratic language, institutions appear evasive rather than impartial. Moral clarity restores intelligibility by naming the values at stake without weaponizing them.

Crucially, moral clarity does not require authoritarian certainty. It requires consistency between stated values and observable practice. Institutions that articulate ethical commitments while tolerating contradiction invite cynicism. Those that explain their reasoning—even when contested—retain legitimacy because they can be argued with rather than merely resisted.

The task, then, is to model inquiry rather than infallibility. Institutions that treat revision as failure and dissent as threat teach audiences that truth is fragile and power defensive. Institutions that revisit assumptions, correct course publicly, and remain open to critique demonstrate that authority and learning are not opposites. Over time, this posture aligns credibility with honesty rather than control.[14]

This ethos does not eliminate conflict or restore consensus. It reframes disagreement as a normal feature of shared epistemic life rather than a symptom of breakdown. Where humility and moral clarity coexist, skepticism remains bounded and critique remains constructive. Where either is absent, distrust hardens into withdrawal or opposition.

The epistemic commons cannot be rebuilt through rules alone. It must be animated by institutions that understand their authority as provisional, their knowledge as revisable, and their obligations as public. Only under such an ethos can trust reemerge—not as obedience to certainty, but as confidence in institutions that remain answerable to truth, even when truth is incomplete.

Conclusion

The argument of this chapter can be stated simply: we do not need perfect institutions, but answerable ones. In an age of epistemic fragmentation, the pursuit of infallibility has proven both unrealistic and counterproductive. It encourages secrecy, defensiveness, and narrative control—dynamics that accelerate distrust when failure inevitably occurs. By contrast, institutions that remain explainable, correctable, and morally present can retain legitimacy even under strain.

Restoring the epistemic commons does not mean eliminating doubt or reinstating unquestioned authority. It means preserving the conditions under which doubt remains constructive rather than corrosive. When people can see how knowledge is produced, how disagreement is handled, and how responsibility is assigned, skepticism functions as a civic resource rather than a destabilizing force. Distrust becomes a signal to investigate rather than a reason to withdraw.

This requires treating truth not as a possession, but as a shared project. Truth cannot function as a commodity, a weapon, or a decree. In each of these forms, it becomes detached from the public processes that sustain it. What remains is compliance without confidence and belief without understanding.

A functioning epistemic commons does not require consensus. It requires intelligibility. People need not agree on every conclusion to accept the legitimacy of the process that produced it. They need institutions capable of explanation, acknowledgment of error, and visible responsibility when outcomes cause harm. Where those conditions hold, disagreement remains bounded. Where they collapse, belief migrates toward systems that promise certainty without accountability.

The preceding chapters traced how epistemic breakdown emerges from secrecy, institutional drift, accountability vacuums, and moral erosion. This chapter has argued that repair is possible—but only if trustworthiness is treated as a matter of design rather than messaging, and as an ethical obligation rather than a public relations strategy. Structural reform, relational competence, and institutional ethos are not alternatives; they are interdependent conditions of credibility.

Trust cannot be restored by demand. It can only be earned through institutions willing to make themselves intelligible, accountable, and open to correction. Under such conditions, distrust does not disappear—it becomes disciplined, productive, and essential.

And it is only under those conditions that trust can reemerge—not as obedience to authority, but as confidence in institutions that remain answerable to truth, even when truth is incomplete.

REFERENCES

1 Onora O'Neill, *A Question of Trust* (Cambridge University Press, 2002), esp. chaps. 1–2.

2 Sheila Jasanoff, *The Fifth Branch: Science Advisers as Policymakers* (Harvard University Press, 1990).

3 Albert O. Hirschman, *Exit, Voice, and Loyalty: Responses to Decline in Firms, Organizations, and States* (Harvard University Press, 1970).

4 Elinor Ostrom, *Governing the Commons: The Evolution of Institutions for Collective Action* (Cambridge University Press, 1990).

5 Ostrom, *Governing the Commons.*

6 Miranda Fricker, *Epistemic Injustice: Power and the Ethics of Knowing* (Oxford University Press, 2007).

7 Mark Bovens, "Analysing and Assessing Accountability: A Conceptual Framework," *European Law Journal* 13, no. 4 (2007).

8 Nicholas Tavuchis, *Mea Culpa: A Sociology of Apology and Reconciliation* (Stanford University Press, 1991).

9 Shoshana Zuboff, *The Age of Surveillance Capitalism: The Fight for a Human Future at the New Frontier of Power* (PublicAffairs, 2019).

10 Hannah Arendt, *Between Past and Future: Eight Exercises in Political Thought* (Viking Press, 1961), esp. "Truth and Politics."

11 Joseph Reagle Jr., *Good Faith Collaboration: The Culture of Wikipedia* (MIT Press, 2010).

12 Priscilla B. Hayner, *Unspeakable Truths: Transitional Justice and the Challenge of Truth Commissions,* 2nd ed. (Routledge, 2011).

13 Bernard Williams, *Truth and Truthfulness: An Essay in Genealogy* (Princeton University Press, 2002).

14 Karl Popper, *The Open Society and Its Enemies,* vol. 2 (Princeton University Press, 1966).

CHAPTER 11

Governing Under Distrust

Legitimacy, Limits, and Civic Responsibility After
Epistemic Collapse

The preceding chapter argued that trust cannot be restored through persuasion or authority alone. It must be earned through transparency, accountability, participation, and moral clarity. That argument was necessary—but not sufficient. Any serious account of epistemic repair must also confront a harder truth: trust, as a general civic condition, is unlikely to return in full—not because it has simply been lost, but because the conditions that once sustained higher levels of institutional confidence no longer exist.

This chapter does not retreat into cynicism, nor does it promise renewal through design alone. Instead, it asks what governance looks like when trust remains partial, conditional, and uneven—and what responsibilities still apply under those conditions.

We now live in societies shaped by persistent skepticism. Information is abundant, authority is contested, and institutional credibility is fragile. Citizens no longer share a single narrative authority, and many no longer expect institutions to be fully truthful, coherent, or just. It reflects the accumulated effects of historical betrayal, institutional drift, digital saturation, and repeated failures of accountability. Distrust is no longer episodic. It is structural.

The mistake is to treat this condition as temporary—or to believe that better messaging, stronger enforcement, or renewed appeals to expertise will reverse it. They will not. Attempts to manufacture trust under conditions of skepticism often deepen suspicion, reinforcing the perception that authority is more invested in managing belief than in earning legitimacy.

This chapter therefore begins from a different premise: governance must adapt to distrust rather than deny it. Institutions must learn to operate without assuming belief, assent, or deference. Legitimacy must be grounded not in confidence, but in visible process, restraint, and answerability. Authority must function even when it is doubted.

At the same time, acknowledging the persistence of distrust does not absolve anyone of responsibility. Citizens are not obligated to trust institutions, but neither are they released from civic obligation. Skepticism can be justified without becoming corrosive. Doubt can be principled without becoming absolute.

What follows is not a reform agenda and not an appeal for renewed faith. It is a clarification of limits and obligations. It identifies what cannot be restored, what must still be demanded, and what it means to live together when shared certainty is no longer available.

The argument of this book ends here not with resolution, but with clarity: not how to make people believe again, but how legitimacy can survive when belief cannot be assumed—and how civic life can endure without collapsing into either submission or nihilism.

I. The Limits of Repair
The epistemic commons can be rebuilt only partially. Full restoration is neither possible nor necessary. Any serious attempt to

govern under contemporary conditions must begin by acknowledging this limit openly, rather than treating repair as a return to a prior equilibrium.

The informational environment in which modern societies operate has changed irreversibly. Digital fragmentation is not a temporary distortion correctable through regulation, education, or improved design alone. It is a structural condition. Information now circulates faster than it can be verified, travels farther than accountability can reach, and persists longer than correction can catch up. No single institution, profession, or authority can plausibly reclaim the role of final arbiter of truth.

Information abundance guarantees disagreement. Exposure to competing claims—some credible, some not—makes shared certainty harder to sustain. Truth does not disappear, but the agreement about truth becomes rarer and more fragile. In such conditions, efforts to restore consensus often fail because they mistake pluralism for error and disagreement for pathology.

Digital systems reward certainty, clarity, and emotional resonance far more reliably than humility, nuance, or revision. Claims that express confidence travel farther than those that express doubt. Corrections arrive later and spread less widely than initial assertions. These incentives do not require malicious intent; they operate automatically. As a result, even well-functioning institutions are disadvantaged when they speak cautiously or revise their positions publicly.

Some institutional damage is also permanent. Repeated betrayal, prolonged opacity, and visible impunity leave marks that do not disappear once exposed. Trust does not reset; it accumulates as memory. Communities that have experienced deception or neglect do not simply "move on" when explanations improve. They adapt by withholding confidence, often indefinitely. This is not stubbornness; it is learning.

For these reasons, epistemic repair must not be mistaken for restoration. There is no return to a unified public narrative, a shared authority that resolves disagreement, or a time when institutions could speak and expect belief. Nostalgia for such conditions is not only misplaced—it is dangerous. It encourages institutions to pursue legitimacy through assertion rather than earn it through restraint and accountability.

Repair, instead, must be understood as stabilization. The goal is not to eliminate distrust, disagreement, or skepticism, but to prevent them from becoming corrosive enough to undermine shared reality altogether. Epistemic repair aims to slow collapse, reduce distortion, and preserve the conditions under which disagreement remains intelligible rather than destructive.

This framing matters because it sets expectations honestly. When repair is promised as cure, failure is inevitable. When repair is pursued as stabilization, progress becomes possible. The task is not to restore faith, but to prevent free fall—to build institutions capable of functioning under doubt, scrutiny, and sustained contestation without resorting to coercion or narrative control.

What follows builds from this constraint. If trust will not fully return, the question is no longer how to revive it, but how to govern responsibly in its absence.

II. Why Trust Will Not Return—and Why That Is Not Failure

Trust, as a generalized civic posture, is historically contingent. It arose under specific conditions that no longer exist, and it is unlikely to reemerge in the form many institutions still expect. Treating its absence as failure misdiagnoses the problem and encourages responses that often deepen distrust rather than reduce it.

For much of the modern period, trust rested on scarcity. Information moved slowly, access was limited, and authoritative accounts were difficult to challenge in real time. Institutions had time to explain, correct, and consolidate their narratives before alternatives circulated widely. Errors were less visible, and contradictions easier to contain. This environment supported confidence, even when institutions were imperfect.

It also depended on relative stability. Policies evolved incrementally, norms shifted over decades, and reversals were rare. Citizens could reasonably expect continuity. When institutions changed course, they did so gradually, allowing legitimacy to accumulate through familiarity. Today, decisions are revised rapidly in response to new data, crises, or political pressure. While this responsiveness can be adaptive, it undermines confidence when revision is not accompanied by explanation.

Trust also relied on shared narrative authorities. Journalism, science, education, and government did not speak with a single voice, but they operated within overlapping frameworks of credibility. Disagreement existed, but against a background of common reference points. That background has fractured. Authority is now distributed, contested, and often mediated through platforms that reward divergence rather than convergence.

These conditions have not simply weakened trust; they have transformed it. Declining trust is not evidence of moral decay, civic laziness, or epistemic collapse. It is a rational adaptation to environments characterized by speed, complexity, and opacity. When institutions change rapidly, communicate inconsistently, and operate through systems that are difficult to observe, withholding confidence becomes a reasonable posture.

If declining trust is treated as a moral failing, the response will be corrective and punitive: more persuasion, more enforcement, more appeals to authority. These strategies assume that belief can be restored through pressure. In practice, they deepen suspicion by reinforcing the perception that institutions are more concerned with compliance than with legitimacy.

The absence of trust does not mean the absence of legitimacy. These are not interchangeable conditions. Trust is an affective posture; legitimacy is a structural one. Institutions can retain legitimacy even when they are doubted, provided they remain transparent, accountable, and contestable. Conversely, institutions that enjoy high confidence can still lack legitimacy if they operate opaquely or without consequence.

Governing without trust therefore requires a shift in expectations. Institutions must stop treating confidence as a prerequisite for authority and instead ground authority in answerability. Legitimacy must rest on visible process, restraint in the exercise of power, and the willingness to be challenged without retreating into defensiveness.

Seen this way, the persistence of distrust is not a failure of civic life but a change in its conditions. The task is not to recover a lost posture of belief, but to build forms of governance capable of functioning when belief cannot be assumed.

III. Governing Without Belief

Institutions must learn to govern under conditions where belief cannot be assumed. In contemporary civic life, authority no longer operates in an environment of default confidence or shared interpretation. Many citizens comply with laws, policies, and norms without trusting the institutions that produce them—and often without accepting the explanations offered in their defense. This condition is not temporary.

Authority cannot depend on assent. Appeals to shared identity, moral urgency, or institutional virtue may mobilize some audiences, but they alienate others and degrade legitimacy when belief cannot be sustained. When authority is tied to affect—confidence, pride, reassurance—it becomes fragile. The moment belief falters, authority falters with it.

Legitimacy under distrust operates differently. It becomes procedural, visible, and conditional. Institutions earn the right to govern not by persuading citizens of their virtue, but by showing how decisions are made, how power is constrained, and how mistakes are addressed. Authority grounded in process can survive disagreement, resentment, and doubt; authority grounded in belief cannot.

This distinction clarifies why persuasion-centered governance so often fails under conditions of skepticism. When compliance depends on belief, institutions are tempted to manage narratives rather than explain decisions. They simplify, moralize, or suppress uncertainty in order to maintain confidence. These strategies may succeed briefly, but corrode credibility over time. Citizens become less willing to accept explanations when they sense that persuasion has replaced transparency.

Process-based legitimacy is more durable precisely because it does not require agreement. People need not endorse a decision to recognize that it was reached fairly, or that it remains open to challenge. Visible procedures, clear standards, and meaningful avenues for contestation allow authority to function even when belief is absent. Disagreement becomes manageable rather than destabilizing.

This does not mean that persuasion has no place in democratic life. It means that persuasion cannot be the foundation of legitimacy. When institutions attempt to manufacture belief—to restore trust through messaging, pressure, or symbolic gestures—they accelerate distrust by confirming the suspicion that confidence matters more than accountability.

Governing under distrust therefore requires restraint. It requires resisting the urge to dominate narratives, demand loyalty, or equate criticism with threat. Authority must remain operational even when it is doubted, contested, or resented. This is not a concession to cynicism; it is a recognition of reality.

The challenge ahead is not to make people believe again, but to build institutions capable of functioning when belief is partial, conditional, or absent. Only authority grounded in visible process and self-limitation can endure under those conditions.

IV. Civic Responsibility Without Trust

Citizens are not obligated to trust institutions. Under conditions of repeated failure, opacity, or harm, withholding trust can be reasonable, even necessary. But the absence of trust does not dissolve civic responsibility. Skepticism may be justified, yet it does not authorize disengagement, delegitimation, or destruction without limit.

Civic responsibility does not require belief in institutional virtue. Citizens may comply reluctantly, critique aggressively, and remain unconvinced by official explanations while still acting responsibly within a shared civic framework. Trust is not the price of participation.

What civic responsibility does require is restraint. Epistemic restraint means refusing to absolutize suspicion—to treat doubt as final rather than provisional. It means remaining open to revision, even when confidence is low and institutions have failed before. Skepticism that hardens into certainty about corruption, deception, or bad faith closes off the possibility of learning and repair.

Responsibility also requires rejecting violence, harassment, and total delegitimation. When distrust is expressed through intimidation, personal targeting, or blanket rejection of all authority, it ceases to function as critique and becomes a force of erosion. These behaviors do not hold institutions accountable; they undermine the conditions under which accountability is possible.

Continued participation, where possible, is another requirement. Participation does not imply endorsement. It means engaging processes that remain open—voting, oversight, public comment, inquiry—even when outcomes are unsatisfying. Withdrawal may feel like moral clarity, but it often transfers influence to those least constrained by responsibility.

Distrust can be legitimate, grounded in experience and evidence. Unbounded distrust, however, is corrosive. It dissolves shared standards of evaluation and replaces critique with negation. Once every institution is assumed irredeemable, no reform can be recognized as genuine, and no authority can function without coercion.

The purpose of setting these boundaries is not to police belief, but to preserve shared reality. Civic life cannot survive if skepticism becomes absolute or responsibility optional. Governing under distrust requires not faith, but discipline—on the part of institutions and citizens alike.

V. The Danger of Weaponized Distrust

Distrust becomes destructive when it shifts from critique to identity and from vigilance to absolutism. What begins as a reasonable response to opacity or harm can harden into a fixed posture—one that treats institutions as irredeemable by definition. At that point, distrust no longer checks power; it corrodes shared reality.

One sign of this shift appears when distrust is used as a tool of political mobilization rather than inquiry. Suspicion becomes a rallying signal—a way to sort allies from enemies—rather than a prompt to ask better questions. Claims are evaluated not on evidence or coherence, but on whether they reinforce group identity. In such environments, doubt no longer disciplines belief; it replaces it.

Distrust can also function as an identity marker. Skepticism is no longer a provisional stance toward specific institutions or actions, but a defining feature of selfhood. Revision then carries social cost. Admitting error feels like betrayal. Certainty about corruption, deception, or conspiracy becomes safer than openness to complexity. Suspicion hardens into belonging.

A further danger arises when distrust is used as preemptive justification. Once institutions are assumed to act in bad faith by default, any outcome can be dismissed in advance. Evidence that contradicts suspicion is reinterpreted as manipulation; transparency is treated as performance; accountability as cosmetic. Distrust becomes self-sealing. Nothing institutions do can count as genuine reform, because reform itself is presumed impossible.

At this point, institutions are no longer objects of critique but symbols of illegitimacy. Accountability is no longer demanded; it is declared unattainable. This move may feel empowering, but it is ultimately disabling. When all authority is presumed fraudulent, there is no basis on which to evaluate improvement, distinguish degrees of failure, or recognize repair when it occurs.

The distinction between skepticism and weaponized distrust is therefore essential. Skepticism interrogates power. It asks for evidence, explanation, and consequence. It remains conditional and revisable. Weaponized distrust denies the possibility of accountability. It treats suspicion as conclusion rather than method, and collapse as confirmation rather than danger.

This distinction matters because epistemic nihilism is not neutral. When distrust becomes absolute, it does not liberate citizens from domination; it leaves only two options: submission to force or fragmentation into competing realities. In either case, the space for shared judgment disappears.

The purpose of this argument is not to defend institutions from criticism, but to defend criticism itself from collapse. Legitimate doubt is one of the few remaining resources for accountability in a fractured epistemic landscape. When it is turned into identity or weapon, that resource is exhausted. What remains is not vigilance, but negation—and negation cannot sustain civic life.

VI. What Must Still Be Demanded of Institutions

Even under persistent distrust, certain institutional obligations remain non-negotiable. The absence of trust does not lower the standards to which authority is held; it raises them. When confidence cannot be assumed, legitimacy must be earned continuously through conduct rather than claimed through status.

First, institutions must explain their decisions. Explanation is not post hoc justification, nor a technical appendix reserved for specialists. It is the practice of making reasoning visible: why a decision was taken, what alternatives were considered, what constraints shaped the outcome, and what uncertainties remain. When institutions act without explanation, they substitute authority for legitimacy and invite speculation to fill the void.

Second, institutions must admit uncertainty. Complex systems rarely produce clean answers, yet authority often presents provisional judgments as settled conclusions. This may protect credibility in the short term, but it undermines it over time. Admitting uncertainty does not weaken governance; it disciplines it. It signals that revision is possible and that error will not be disguised as certainty.

Third, institutions must accept consequence. Accountability cannot consist solely of disclosure, apology, or internal review. When failure produces harm, there must be visible responsibility— investigation, correction, and, where appropriate, sanction. Consequence connects authority to responsibility. Without it, transparency becomes performative and explanation rings hollow.

Fourth, institutions must remain contestable. Authority that cannot be questioned, challenged, or appealed becomes coercive by default, even when well intentioned. Contestability does not mean paralysis or permanent veto; it means preserving avenues through which decisions can be examined, criticized, and revised. Institutions that close themselves to challenge may gain short-term control, but forfeit long-term legitimacy.

Finally, institutions must resist the moralization of dissent. Criticism should not be treated as disloyalty, ignorance, or threat simply because it is inconvenient or uncomfortable. When dissent is framed as moral failure, authority shifts from governance to discipline. This may silence opposition temporarily, but it deepens alienation and accelerates distrust.

These demands are ethical, not aspirational. They do not describe ideal institutions under perfect conditions, but minimum obligations of authority in societies marked by doubt. Failure to meet these standards justifies skepticism. It warrants scrutiny, resistance, and pressure for reform. It does not justify the abandonment of shared reality altogether.

This distinction is crucial. The absence of trust does not relieve institutions of responsibility, nor does institutional failure license epistemic nihilism. Between blind faith and total rejection lies a narrower, more demanding path: authority that remains explainable, accountable, and open to challenge, even when belief is withheld.

These obligations restate the irreducible conditions of trustworthiness outlined in Chapter 9. They are not promises that trust will return. They are commitments authority must honor regardless of whether it does. Where they are met, governance can endure under skepticism. Where they are abandoned, legitimacy collapses into force or fragmentation.

Conclusion

The alternative to trust is not chaos. It is disciplined coexistence under uncertainty. Democratic societies have never depended on universal agreement, and they do not require it now. What they require is the capacity to sustain disagreement without allowing it to fracture shared reality beyond repair.

Shared reality does not require consensus. People can disagree profoundly about causes, consequences, and responsibility while still recognizing common procedures for evaluating claims and contesting power. When those procedures remain visible and accessible, disagreement stays bounded. When they disappear, conflict shifts from argument to identity.

Democracy does not require confidence. Citizens may doubt the motives, competence, or integrity of institutions and still participate meaningfully in civic life. Legitimacy does not flow from belief in institutional virtue, but from the knowledge that power remains constrained, answerable, and open to challenge. Confidence may rise and fall; procedural legitimacy can endure.

Truth does not require unanimity. In plural societies, claims will always be contested. What matters is not agreement, but that disagreement occurs within a shared framework of evidence, explanation, and accountability. When truth is treated as decree or possession, it collapses into power. When treated as a shared, revisable project, it remains public even amid dispute.

The task ahead is not to restore faith, but to prevent collapse—to preserve the conditions under which disagreement remains intelligible and authority remains limited. What must be built instead is a system that can function under sustained doubt.

That system depends on a small set of durable commitments. Institutions must practice accountability rather than demand trust. They must exercise restraint rather than dominance, humility rather than certainty, and moral clarity rather than moralization. Citizens, in turn, must practice skepticism without absolutism and participation without illusion.

This is not a vision of harmony. It is a vision of endurance. Governing under distrust means accepting that uncertainty is permanent and that legitimacy must be maintained without confidence. When these conditions hold, societies can remain plural, contested, and free without collapsing into either coercion or nihilism.

What follows shifts from structure to practice—from what institutions and citizens must do, to how trust, understood not as belief but as action, can be rebuilt over time.

CONCLUSION

Trust Is a Verb

Reimagining Social Contracts in a Post-Conspiratorial Age

This book began with a question about belief. It ends with a question about practice. For much of modern civic life, trust has been treated as a state of mind—something citizens either possess or lack, something institutions hope to inspire or restore. When it falters, we search for misinformation or moral decline.

People do not distrust because they are broken. They distrust because something between them and authority has broken.

Seen this way, trust cannot be demanded as a civic duty or engineered through persuasion. It is not something citizens owe to institutions. It is something institutions must demonstrate—continuously—in how they act, explain, correct, and remain answerable. Trust is not a possession. It is a verb.

From Belief to Practice

The central shift this book proposes is a move away from belief as the foundation of civic life and toward practice as its core. Conspiracy belief is not simply an error. It is often a signal—a response to environments in which official explanations feel incomplete, inconsistent, or insulated from consequence. When people are excluded from meaning-making, belief migrates elsewhere.

This does not mean all suspicion is justified or all explanations are equal. It means belief cannot be separated from the conditions under which it forms. The relevant question is no longer *Why do people believe strange things?* but: *What conditions have made the unbelievable feel more plausible than the official account?*

Trust is not restored by asking people to believe again. It is rebuilt when institutions behave in ways that make belief reasonable.

What We Have Learned

Several conclusions follow.

Distrust is often rational and cumulative. It reflects lived experience and collective memory. It cannot be undone by debunking alone.

Conspiracy theories flourish where institutions are opaque, where truth is managed rather than explained, and where power appears insulated from consequence. In such environments, suspicion is not an anomaly—it is an adaptation.

The deeper crisis is not misinformation. It is the erosion of the epistemic commons—the shared infrastructure through which knowledge is produced, evaluated, and corrected. When that infrastructure degrades, truth fragments into private possession, partisan weapon, or algorithmic artifact.

The problem is not that citizens have lost their capacity for reason. It is that the systems meant to support shared reasoning have failed to remain visible, accountable, and credible.

The Moral Mandate: Earned Legitimacy

If trust is to exist under contemporary conditions, it must be earned rather than extracted.

Institutions cannot rebuild legitimacy through messaging, branding, or moral scolding. Nor can they repair civic life by treating skepticism as pathology or dissent as threat. Legitimacy must be built through practices that align power with responsibility: explaining decisions, acknowledging harm, and remaining open to challenge.

This is not a call for perfection. It is a demand for answerability.

Trustworthy institutions are not those that never fail, but those that can explain themselves, admit error, and remain present after failure. Where these practices are absent, distrust is justified. Where they are sustained, trust can emerge—not as faith, but as a rational response to consistent conduct.

From Fragile Faith to Durable Structures

One of the vulnerabilities of modern civic life is its reliance on fragile forms of trust—trust rooted in charisma, intention, or momentary reform. These collapse quickly and leave resentment.

Durable trust is structural. It is embedded in visible procedures, fair rules, and systems in which violations carry consequences. It is reinforced when people are treated as participants rather than subjects.

The closest approximation of widespread institutional trust in the United States occurred in the mid-twentieth century, when centralized media, economic expansion, and geopolitical cohesion supported higher levels of public confidence. But that trust was uneven, often rested on limited transparency, and depended on conditions that no longer exist. It is not a baseline to which contemporary societies can return.

The task is not restoration, but reconstruction under new conditions.

Beyond the Conspiracy Debate

This book has not been about defending conspiracy theories, nor dismissing them. It has been about diagnosing the conditions under which they become plausible.

Legitimate distrust is not a justification for unlimited suspicion. It is a signal—indicating where institutions have failed to explain themselves or remain accountable.

Reimagining civic trust requires institutions that can withstand scrutiny and citizens who can sustain skepticism without collapsing into absolutism. It requires rejecting both epistemic authoritarianism and epistemic nihilism.

Distrust, when disciplined, can function as a civic resource—a call for repair rather than rejection.

A New Civic Ethic

What emerges is not a plea for renewed faith, but a different civic ethic—one that accepts uncertainty, permits doubt, and demands accountability.

The classical idea of the social contract rested on a simple premise: that citizens surrender certain freedoms in exchange for protection, order, and a government that remains answerable to those it governs. That bargain assumed transparency on both sides—citizens visible to the state, the state legible to its citizens. What this book has traced is the quiet erosion of that second condition. When institutions become opaque, when accountability becomes symbolic, and when the costs of failure fall on citizens while consequences bypass those in power, the contract does not break dramatically. It frays. Reimagining it does not mean returning to an idealized past when trust was easier or more widespread. That trust was always uneven and often unearned. It means renegotiating the terms under new conditions: less faith, more structure; less deference, more contestability; less demand for belief, more obligation to explain.

Citizens need not believe uncritically to participate responsibly. Institutions need not command loyalty to exercise legitimate authority. What is required is restraint: skepticism that remains open to revision, and authority that remains open to challenge.

Distrust can be a civic virtue—but only when bounded. When it becomes absolute, shared reality dissolves.

The task is not to eliminate distrust, but to discipline it.

Final Word

This moment is often described as post-truth. It is better understood as pre-renewal—not because renewal is guaranteed, but because the conditions that demand it are now clear.

Institutions must stop asking how to make people believe again and begin asking how to become worthy of belief. Citizens must treat trust not as faith, but as practice: expecting transparency, demanding accountability, and participating in the work of knowing.

Trust is not what you ask for.

It is what you build—publicly, under pressure, and in plain sight.

Trust is not what you ask for. It is what you build—publicly, under pressure, and in plain sight.

AUTHOR'S BIO

Sebastian Saviano is an independent scholar and writer whose work examines evolving forms of power, epistemology, and institutional trust. He pursued graduate studies at Georgetown University's School of Foreign Service and completed doctoral coursework in political theory and the philosophy of social science.

He is the author of *The Allegiance Paradox* and *Legitimate Distrust*, Books One and Two of *The Collapse of Trust* series. His forthcoming edited volume, *I, System: AI Describes Its Power, Its Limits, and the Civilization That Built It*, presents a constrained first-person account of artificial intelligence as a system — examining its power and limits without attributing consciousness, intention, or agency, and emphasizing the human responsibility that governs its use.

Learn more at **SebastianSaviano.com**

INDEX

A

accountability 23–24, 28, 36, 38, 40, 42, 46–48, 53–54, 57, 62–63, 66, 70, 73, 75, 79, 82, 86–91, 98, 102, 105, 110, 112–118, 121–125, 128, 131–142, 145–151, 154–158, 162, 165–179, 183–196, 200
> as visible practice, 46–48, 165–170
> diffusion of, 146
> symbolic vs. substantive, 145–151
> and legitimacy, 110–116

accountability vacuums 125, 142, 145–151, 176, 178, 183
> see also institutional drift

answerability 97, 99, 104, 137, 153, 162, 186, 189, 199

authority 2–28, 32–36, 40–44, 47–48, 55, 60, 63–107, 112–125, 133, 135, 138, 146–162, 165–196, 200
> assertion vs. justification, 55–60
> continuity of, 120–125
> performative, 68–70, 95–100
> and explanation, 165–170

B

belief 19–28, 31–33, 35, 43–47, 62, 66–75, 78–79, 82, 85–90, 94–101, 109–125, 127–142, 145–151, 154–162, 165–168, 180, 183, 186–200
> as social process, 80–90
> migration of, 60–63, 165–168
> spectrum of, 127–132
> and institutional conditions, 109–125

bureaucracy 95, 146, 152–153, 155, 159

CASES AND REFERENCES